At Issue

| Charter Schools

Other Books in the At Issue Series:

At Issue

|Charter Schools

Diane Andrews Henningfeld, Book Editor

GREENHAVEN PRESS

An imprint of Thomson Gale, a part of The Thomson Corporation

ST. PETERSBURG COLLEGE

Detroit • New York • San Francisco • New Haven, Conn. • Waterville, Maine • London

Christine Nasso, *Publisher*
Elizabeth Des Chenes, *Managing Editor*

© 2008 The Gale Group.

Star logo is a trademark and Gale and Greenhaven Press are registered trademarks used herein under license.

For more information, contact:
Greenhaven Press
27500 Drake Rd.
Farmington Hills, MI 48331-3535
Or you can visit our Internet site at http://www.gale.com

LIBRARY OF CONGRESS CATALOGING-IN-PUBLICATION DATA

Charter schools / Diane Andrews Henningfeld, book editor.
    p. cm. -- (At issue)
Includes bibliographical references and index.
ISBN-13: 978-0-7377-3914-5 (hardcover)
ISBN-13: 978-0-7377-3915-2 (pbk.)
1. Charter schools--United States--Juvenile literature. I. Henningfeld, Diane Andrews.
  LB2806.36.C5353 2008
  371.01--dc22

                                                    2007038578

ISBN-10: 0-7377-3914-2 (hardcover)
ISBN-10: 0-7377-3915-0 (pbk.)

Printed in the United States of America
10 9 8 7 6 5 4 3 2 1

Contents

Introduction

The charter school movement has grown and gained strength from 1997 to 2007. Although they are publicly funded, charters are freed from many of the rules and regulations binding traditional public schools in an attempt to increase student achievement. While teachers themselves have started up many charter schools, teachers are also some of the most vociferous critics of the charter school movement. A close look at the relationship between teachers and charter schools reveals why this movement is such a hotly debated issue.

Teacher training and experience are two important points of disagreement between the opponents and proponents of charter schools. Traditionally, in order to be certified as a teacher, a person must have completed a college degree in education. Regular public schools require that every teacher must be certified. However, in many states, charter schools are able to hire noncertified teachers.

Opponents of charter schools argue that uncertified teachers are unqualified teachers. They warn that an influx of uncertified teachers into a school will lead to less effective teaching and, consequently, to less student learning. The National Education Association reports, "[T]he scores of students taught by uncertified teachers in charter schools were significantly lower than those of charter school students with certified teachers." A corollary to this concern is the relative inexperience of charter school teachers in comparison to traditional public school teachers. Multiple studies affirm that far more teachers in charters are in their first years of teaching than are the faculty at regular public schools. Opponents of charter schools are troubled by these statistics. They believe that the best teachers are ones with the most experience in handling not only the subject matter in a class but also the day-to-day classroom experience, including discipline. The National Education Association reports, "Charter school students with inexperienced teachers did significantly worse than students in traditional public schools with less experienced teachers."

However, according to the writers of *Hopes, Fears, and Realities: A Balanced Look at American Charter Schools in 2006*, charter school leaders affirm "their belief in individual schools' need to hire whomever they choose and to pay teachers based on performance and demand for skills, rather than on seniority." Proponents of charter schools further argue that the brightest and best college students are attracted to charter school teaching. Supporters believe that having teachers better prepared in their individual disciplines and from the most competitive universities and colleges will lead to improved teaching and student achievement. A study conducted by the Educational Policy Center at Michigan State University in 2004, for example, demonstrated that at that time, 35 percent of the teachers at charter schools had graduated from more selective colleges while only 29 percent of teachers at traditional public schools had graduated from more selective colleges. As for experience, charter school proponents claim that young teachers are less jaded and more enthusiastic. These qualities inspire young people to achieve more. In addition, charter school proponents assert, charter school teachers quickly gain the experience they need to be highly effective teachers.

A second important area to consider is unionization and teacher satisfaction. In traditional public education, teachers are generally members of teachers' unions that negotiate their contracts, provide benefits, and protect their jobs. Teachers find more satisfaction in their positions, unions argue, when they are not worried about job security. Educational researchers Robin J. Lake and Paul T. Hill write: "Union leaders thought professionalism was best served by delineating clear roles, work rules, rights, and responsibilities for teachers." Union leaders believe that unionized teachers have more protection to practice academic freedom and introduce innovations into their classes. In addition, the teachers' unions assert, charter schools are being used by politicians and school boards to undercut teachers' salaries and status. They believe that the cost of running the school is more important to charter school administrators than the job satisfaction and morale of teachers.

Charter school backers, though, assert that teachers find *more* satisfaction in charter schools because they are not limited by huge bureaucracies, including unions, that prevent them from implementing new ideas. In addition, because charter schools can set their own rules and regulations regarding student behavior, they are able to improve the overall school atmosphere by holding students to strict standards of behavior as a condition of attendance. Freed from unnecessary rules and regulations, and supported by strong discipline standards, proponents argue, teachers see their students achieve more while they enjoy greater job satisfaction. As educational researcher Caprice Young writes: "If more teachers were free to channel the energy and creativity they currently put into overcoming bureaucratic barriers, I believe we would see a big jump in test scores and a huge decline in the dropout rate. The early data is showing this to be the case as more and more talented school administrators and teachers are starting charter schools."

Both charter school opponents and proponents acknowledge one large problem for charter schools: the rate of teachers leaving (also called the attrition rate) charter schools is much higher than it is at traditional public schools. According to a 2007 study by researchers Gary Miron and Brooks Applegate, about 40 percent of charter teachers who are new to the profession of teaching leave after their first year. At traditional public schools, only about 20 percent of new teachers leave after their first year. Opponents find this statistic indicative of fatal flaws in the charter movement. Proponents simply view it as a challenge to be addressed, arguing that as charter schools mature, the situation will right itself.

The relationship between teachers and charter schools is just one aspect of the charter school debate. Issues concerning teaching, student achievement, closing the achievement gap between majority and minority students, and equitable funding are a few of the topics covered in the viewpoints included in *At Issue: Charter Schools*. With the increasing focus on U.S. schools, it is unlikely that this controversial subject will be resolved in the near future.

Charter Schools: An Overview

Education Week Research Center

The Education Week Research Center is the research arm of Educational Projects in Education, a nonprofit organization that publishes Education Week *and* The Teacher *magazines and maintains the Web site edweek.org.*

Charter schools are public schools, funded by taxpayers, but they are not bound by many of the regulations of traditional public schools. Proponents of charter schools believe that the small size of charter schools leads to better student learning. In addition, charter schools often have innovative curricula. Yet some voice concerns that charter schools cause lackluster student achievement and present the potential for financial mismanagement. There is also the fear that charter schools will drain important resources away from traditional public schools. So far, the evidence is mixed; some studies suggest charter schools are doing a good job while other studies demonstrate that charter schools are failing.

Although they serve only a tiny fraction of the nation's public school students, charter schools have seized a prominent role in education today [in 2007]. They are at the center of a growing movement to challenge traditional notions of what public education means.

Charter schools are by definition independent public schools. Although funded with taxpayer dollars, they operate free from many of the laws and regulations that govern traditional public schools. In exchange for that freedom, they are bound to the terms of a contract or "charter" that lays out a school's mission, academic goals, and accountability procedures. State laws set the parameters for charter contracts, which are overseen by a designated charter school authorizer—often the local school district or related agency.

With their relative autonomy, charter schools are seen as a way to provide greater educational choice and innovation within the public school system. Their founders are often teachers, parents, or activists who feel restricted by traditional public schools. In addition, many charters are run by for-profit companies, forming a key component of the privatization movement in education.

A chief reason for charter schools' appeal is that they are typically smaller than their more traditional counterparts.

The Appeal of Charter Schools

The concept of charter schools clearly has strong appeal. Since the first charter school was founded in Minnesota in 1992, charters have fanned out across the country. According to the Center for Education Reform, an organization that advocates for charters, there were nearly 3,000 charter schools in 37 states and the District of Columbia in January 2004, with particularly high concentrations in some big cities. The schools enroll some 685,000 students. Charters serve the full range of grade levels, often in unique combinations or spans. On the whole, they also appear to enroll a diverse body of students. A 2002 survey report by SRI International, a nonprofit research institute, states that "on average, more than half the students in charter schools were members of ethnic minority groups, 12 percent received special education services, and 6 percent were English language learners."

A chief reason for charter schools' appeal is that they are typically smaller than their more traditional counterparts, advocates say. According to the Center for Education Reform (2002), the average charter school enrollment is 242, compared with 539 in traditional public schools. Researchers—and no doubt parents—link small schools with higher achievement, more individualized instruction, greater safety, and increased student involvement.

Many charter school authorizers have failed to hold charters accountable, leaving some students to languish in low-performing schools.

Another attraction is charters' often specialized and ambitious educational programs. Charters frequently take alternative curricular approaches (e.g., direct instruction or Core Knowledge), emphasize particular fields of study (e.g., the arts or technology), or serve special populations of students (e.g., special education or at-risk students). Recently, with the rise of distance learning, a growing number of "cyber" charter schools have even done away with the concept of an actual bricks-and-mortar school building.

Coupled with aggressive academic goals in charter contracts, such "alternative visions of schooling," according to a 2000 U.S. Department of Education report, are a primary motivating force behind the growth of charter schools.

Concerns About Charter Schools

If charters' independence is central to their appeal, however, it is also a source of concern. Though charters must spell out performance goals in their contracts, some observers question how well academics and student achievement in charters are monitored. A high-profile 2002 report from the American Federation of Teachers, for example, argued that many charter school authorizers have failed to hold charters accountable, leaving some students to languish in low-performing schools.

Likewise, some observers say that charters, by virtue of their autonomy, can be vulnerable to financial problems and mismanagement. Indeed, the fiscal arrangements of charters can be inherently problematic, in part because, in many states, charters' access to facilities and start-up funds is limited.

Skeptics worry that charters unfairly divert resources and policy attention from regular public schools.

Increasingly, such issues are coming to the attention of state leaders. After a series of well-publicized charter closures and compliance problems, some states have begun to re-examine their charter systems with the aim of giving the schools greater oversight. At the same time, many charter supporters remain leery of increased regulation.

Outside of such managerial concerns, some critics have also charged that, on a school-by-school basis, charters are more racially segregated than traditional public schools, thus denying students the educational "benefits of racial and ethnic diversity," [according to the Harvard University Civil Rights Project]. Charter supporters have responded that some charters have high concentrations of minority students because demand for schooling alternatives is highest among such students, whom they say are often poorly served by the traditional public school systems.

Other concerns about charter schools mirror those surrounding their private school choice counterpart—school vouchers. Skeptics worry that charters unfairly divert resources and policy attention from regular public schools. Other observers counter that charters improve existing school systems through choice and competition.

Mixed Results

Meanwhile, the question of whether charters or traditional public schools do a better job of educating students is still open to debate. The research is highly mixed—in part due [to] the complexities of comparison and wide performance differences among charters.

A case in point: One study by Western Michigan University's Evaluation Center found that charter schools in Michigan posted significantly lower scores—and less consistent gains—on state standardized tests than their host districts. Yet, in a later evaluation of charters in Pennsylvania, the center found that "student achievement appears to be a source of modest strength" for the schools, with some making steady test-score gains. That study points to best-practices evaluation and stronger accountability as ways to expand charter schools' gains.

Taken together, other recent studies paint an equally varied portrait. Studies by the Goldwater Institute and California State University–Los Angeles found that students in charter schools show higher growth in achievement than their counterparts in traditional public schools. A major state-commissioned study by the RAND Corp., meanwhile, concluded that charters in California were making solid improvements in student achievement over time and generally keeping pace with other public schools on tests scores after adjustment to reflect students' demographic backgrounds.

By contrast, however, a 2003 study of charter schools in Ohio [by the Legislative Office of Education Oversight] found them falling short of traditional public schools on the majority of comparable performance measures, concluding that charter schools "were doing no better than low-performing traditional public schools with similar demographic characteristics." Likewise, a 2002 study of North Carolina charter schools by the North Carolina Center for Public Policy concluded that charter schools were lagging behind traditional public schools in achievement growth and had not proven themselves to be any "better at serving at-risk students."

Still, that report allows that there is significant variation among charters: "Some schools have delivered on the charter school promise, and some clearly have not," the researchers found. Some charter proponents would argue that such individual examples of achievement may in themselves go a long way toward validating the charter experiment, representing successful new models of schooling that states and parents can build on.

Charter Schools Threaten the Public Education System

New York State PTA

The New York State PTA is an organization of public school parents and teachers who support traditional public school education.

In January 2007, Eliot Spitzer, governor of New York, announced that he would raise the cap on the number of charter schools in the state by 150 percent in spite of the fact that many charter schools are failing. Charter schools threaten traditional public education, because they drain financial resources from traditional public schools and are not subject to local oversight. Therefore, to protect the public schools and students, the Charter School Act must be changed. By law, charter schools should be accessible to all students, subject to the same rules and regulations placed on traditional schools, and funded without charging tuition or fees.

In [New York] Governor [Eliot] Spitzer's Contract for Excellence address [January 26, 2007] he states that charter schools, as models of educational innovation, play an important role in achieving educational excellence. For this reason, the governor's education reform agenda includes a proposal to raise the statewide charter school cap by 150%. This would be enacted by increasing the number of charter schools from 100 to 250 with an allotment of 50 for New York City.

New York State PTA, "Issues Brief: Charter Schools and Talking Points: Charter Schools," *www.nyspta.org,* March 2007, pp. 1–2. www.nyspta.org/pdf/Issues%20Brief %20Charter%20Schools.pdf. Copyright © NYS PTA. Reproduced by permission.

The intent of the NY Charter Schools Act was to allow for the establishment of models of academic innovation that were free of bureaucratic regulation but would be held strictly accountable for their performance. Unfortunately, New York's law funded this experiment by diverting money away from its traditional public schools. While a number of NYC charter schools have met the standard of improving achievement, studies have shown that a majority of charter schools outside the city have failed miserably. In reality, the implementation of the Act has, in certain areas of the state such as Albany, Schenectady, and Buffalo, led to unintended consequences in that these communities are suffering serious financial drain on traditional public school programs and there is no local recourse.

Charter schools . . . must not undermine the opportunity to provide students in traditional public schools with excellence in education and quality of life.

Charter Schools Drain Resources

Fair funding of public education has been a priority of the NYS PTA [New York State Parent Teachers Association]. Our current position, *Funding for Charter Schools*, established in 2001, seeks to address the negative financial impact of charter schools on traditional public schools. The charter school act provides for per pupil funds to be drawn from school district operating expenses; requires that textbooks, transportation, computer software, library materials, and health and welfare services be provided; and, in the event of contingency budgets, the requirement to finance a charter school may result in having to eliminate or cut programs in traditional public schools of a district. Districts take an additional financial hit when students who signed to attend charter schools change their minds and return to the district or if a charter school closes mid-year. Our resolution urges members to support legislation to change the method of funding NY's charter schools in order to eliminate the potential for an adverse effect upon traditional public schools and the communities they are intended to benefit.

Under the Governor's proposal to increase the cap, despite the potential impact on local schools, there is no provision to allow the local board of education or community to review and authorize a charter school application. While the Governor has proposed transition aid to help ease the initial financial impact on school districts hardest hit by their charters, many other communities will receive no transition aid at all. The selection process for allocating transition aid is unclear, and there is no indication of the number of years the aid would be available.

Charter schools are financially devastating the city districts of Buffalo, Schenectady, and Albany.

Requirements for Charter Schools

Governor Spitzer's proposed Executive Budget embraces public education as a state funding priority. With unprecedented funding levels he has taken a bold approach to shaping the future of education for NY's children. NYS PTA acknowledges charter schools as an avenue to school reform and supports actions that rationally invest in innovation and experimentation. It is the hope of the NYS PTA that the allocation of new resources will be invested wisely in initiatives that produce measurable and sustainable gains for all students. To ensure the promise of modeling innovative public education, charter schools must be open to all students, adhere to state and federal laws governing public schools, include meaningful parent involvement, be accountable to local school boards, and be funded in a way that does not undermine the opportunity to provide students in traditional public schools with excellence in education and quality of life.

Problems with Charter Schools

- While a number of NYC charter schools have met the standard of improving achievement, studies have shown that a majority of charter schools outside the city have failed miserably.

- Charter schools are financially devastating the city districts of Buffalo, Schenectady, and Albany.

- The current process of establishing charter schools, and the Governor's proposal to lift the cap, make no provisions for the long-held principle of local control. School district budgets are approved by community residents. Voters currently have no input into the establishment of charter schools that will be diverting funds already approved for traditional public schools. Applications or renewals of charters should be approved by the local school board before being received and acted on by any chartering entity.

- Charter schools drain students and finances from school districts. Charter schools should not enroll more than 5% of a local district's student enrollment nor divert more than 5% of a local district's budget.

- School districts need time to adjust and prepare for the opening of a charter school. A reasonable notice period should be required between the approval of a charter application and the opening of a charter school.

- The Governor's proposal limits transitional charter school aid to be provided only for certain schools; the selection process is undefined and there is no indication of how many years it will be provided. To ease the financial impact of charter schools, transitional state aid must be provided to *any* local district when a new charter school opens as well as to those that already exist.

- There must be a provision for the immediate recovery of funds by a local school district when

a) students who signed up do not attend a charter school;

b) students return to a regular district school from a charter school;

c) a charter school ceases operation before the end of the school year

- Charter schools are financed by a formula based on a school district's prior year's annual operating expense (AOE). However, there are fixed costs that do not decrease when students attend charter schools, such as staffing, utilities, supplies, and insurance. The formula should be revised to hold districts harmless for these fixed costs and reflect the difference between per pupil costs for K-8 (90%) and secondary (110%) students.

- School districts placed on a contingency budget may not increase their budget beyond the cap imposed by the state. However, districts must still pay the charter school at the prior year's AOE. This potentially forces the district to eliminate or reduce programs and services in traditional public schools. Contingency budget constraints should apply to funding that flows to charter schools, not only to funding that flows to traditional public schools.

What Charter Schools Should Be

Not all charter schools hold to the following NYS PTA beliefs that charter schools:

- Be open to all students with limited English proficiency, students with special needs, and students from diverse racial and cultural backgrounds.

- Comply with federal and state laws governing public schools, including laws regarding teacher qualifications, testing standards, and fiscal accountability.

- Adhere to federal, state, and local school boards in the districts where they are located.

- Be accountable to local school boards in the districts where they are located.

- Be funded in such a way as to preclude the charging of tuitions or mandatory fees not charged by other public schools in the district.

- Be independent of nonpublic, sectarian, religious, or home-based school affiliations.

- Include parents in meaningful decision-making roles.

3

Charter Schools Do Not Threaten the Public Education System

James Forman Jr.

James Forman Jr., a law professor at Georgetown University College of Law, writes on law and education and is the cofounder of the Maya Angelou Public Charter School.

Public school supporters often see charter schools as a threat to traditional public education for two important reasons. First, they fear that charter schools will "cream-skim" the best students away from struggling public schools. Second, they fear that charters will drain much-needed resources away from public schools. Recent data, however, demonstrate that charters do not cream-skim and that students from all races, classes, and ability are more or less equally divided between charter and traditional public schools. Moreover, charter schools, because they rely on unstable private support, could become important allies for public schools in demanding more funding for all public education.

In America, as in much of the world, government increasingly relies on non-government actors, including private firms, to achieve public ends. This has sparked controversy across various sectors, and nowhere more passionately than in the field of education. Of the market-based reforms in education, charter schools have had the greatest impact. By the

James Forman Jr., "Do Charter Schools Threaten Public Education? Emerging Evidence from Fifteen Years of a Quasi-Market for Schooling," *University of Illinois Law Review*, vol. 2007, May 2007, pp. 1–3, 22–23, 26–28, 30–32, 35–36. http://home.law.uiuc.edu/lrev/publications/2000s/2007/2007_3/Forman.pdf. Copyright © 2007 The Board of Trustees of the University of Illinois. Reproduced by permission.

2004–2005 school year, there were approximately 3,000 charter schools in 40 states and the District of Columbia, and governments face continued pressure to expand that number. In some cities the pace of growth has been especially quick: Charter schools enroll more than 25% of the students in Dayton, OH, and almost 25% in Washington, DC and Kansas City, MO.

Traditional Public Schools Fear "Cream-Skimming"

Charter schools—and the market-based arguments often made for them—are seen by some as threatening traditional public schools. One of the central fears motivating charter skeptics is typically referred to as "cream-skimming." A choice system, critics have long suggested, would privilege those students and parents whose race, class, or educational background left them better positioned to navigate the market for schools. Similarly, schools would have an incentive to recruit students whose educational ability and family backgrounds made them attractive. At the end of the day, the traditional public system would be left populated by the least able children with the least active parents. So even if choice benefited individual families, society as a whole, and especially disadvantaged families, would suffer.

The fear of cream-skimming is connected to the other fundamental fear of public school supporters—that schools will lose political clout as more advantaged families depart the traditional public system. Similarly, some public school supporters worry that charter schools, over time, will undermine the legitimacy of public authority and reduce citizen engagement on behalf of the public system. As [scholar] Bruce Fuller has suggested, "charter school founders—leading their human-scale institutions, and, in the aggregate, the charge to decentralize government—may paradoxically erode the strength of public authority and the very agencies on which their local livelihood depends." Stated more broadly, the question is whether charters will tilt the balance toward government for the pursuit of individual interests and away from the common good? Given the move towards privatization across industries and the hostility of many policymakers to a robust state, do charter schools undermine the notion that providing high-quality schooling for all children is a core public responsibility?

Nationally, it appears that the students who attend charters and district public schools are of roughly equal academic ability.

Passionate Arguments

Many of the participants argue with great passion. [University of Wisconsin–Milwaukee professor] Alex Molnar, for example, claims that the goal of many powerful charter school advocates "is not nearly as caring as their rhetoric. Bluntly put, it is to dismember public education and feed off the carcass." Similarly, National Education Association President Reg Weaver warns parents to be careful of "the voucherizers, the privatizers, the charterizers who will come and try to fool our communities, saying this is best for your kid. [T]hey're not coming with solutions for all of our children. They might be coming with solutions for one or two or three but not for the vast majority." In many respects the intensity of the debate is predictable. After all, if the proper role of government is a matter of great interest to Americans, nowhere is that more the case than with schooling. Education has long been viewed as the ultimate guarantor of equal opportunity for all Americans and has played a central role in the struggle for racial equality.

The intensity of the rhetoric, however, masks the reality that, especially in the early years, nobody knew the answers to some key questions. The first charter law passed in Minnesota in 1991; because charter schools were so new, the absence of data inherently limited the debate. In the scheme of American educational policy history, charter schools are still [as of 2007] relatively novel. I do not suggest that we know enough today to resolve all the questions I have described. But we do have substantial additional data upon which to draw. Charter schools have expanded rapidly, and interest from researchers has remained high. The last few years especially have seen an outpouring of empirical and other research touching on issues central to the charter experiment. . . .

Cream-Skimming Hypothesis Is Not Confirmed

I would suggest that the evidence to date—while not unequivocal—does not confirm the cream-skimming hypothesis. For race, blacks are disproportionately in charters, whites are disproportionately in traditional public schools, and Hispanics are fairly evenly distributed between the two. These findings should matter to those who believe that white flight to charters combined with the "green follows white" principle [the theory that rich, white students receive more funding than poor, black students] will diminish support for district schools. Looking at class measures, poor students are distributed fairly equally between the two types of schools. And turning to other measures of privilege, the evidence, while limited, does not point strongly in either direction. Nationally, it appears that the students who attend charters and district public schools are of roughly equal academic ability; more educated parents choose charters in North Carolina; and charter parents are no more or less engaged in their children's education in Washington, DC.

However, it would be a mistake to suggest, as some charter school proponents have recently done [as of May 2007], that charter schools in fact serve a more disadvantaged population of students. First of all, other than attracting a greater proportion of black students, there is no dimension where evidence has established that charter schools consistently draw less privileged students. Moreover, charter school advocates eager to rebut claims of cream-skimming (and eager to explain un-inspiring academic achievement results) overlook the fact that the demographic make-up of the schools could change. State and federal studies of charter student demographics have found varying enrollment patterns over time, which is not surprising given that the market is new and growing rapidly.

Indeed, it is worth watching whether the federal No Child Left Behind (NCLB) legislation increases cream-skimming by charters, especially at the high school level. Under NCLB, high schools—including charters—are judged by the percentage of their 10th graders who pass state tests. Each year, an increasing percentage of 10th graders must meet state proficiency levels for the school to satisfy federal requirements. Under federal law, schools are not judged based on how much each student's test scores improve while the student is at that school. Instead, a school is thought to have improved if this year's 10th grade class does better than last year's. This regime gives a school two choices. It can teach better—and for high schools this means teaching better in the 9th grade and first half of 10th grade, since the tests upon which the entire school is judged are given mid-way through the sophomore year. Or the school can try to recruit students who enter the 9th grade with higher test scores, because they are more likely to test well 18 months later. Because schools are just beginning to face significant sanctions for repeatedly failing to meet federal standards, it is too early to tell whether charter schools will respond with increased cream-skimming. But the law creates incentives for them to do so. . . .

Critics Fear Loss of Funding

Critics of school choice argue that the long-term impact will be to undermine support for funding district schools. At firstblush, the claim might seem to depend entirely on char-ters having a cream-skimming impact—in other words, if the more privileged parents and their political capital leave the charters for district schools, then district schools will have less support. In this formulation, the argument would be considerably weakened, and perhaps repudiated in full, by the absence of cream-skimming effects. . . . But there is another way to state the funding argument, which is independent of cream-skimming. To the extent that charter schools are predicated on the notion that they can achieve better results with the same or less money than district schools receive, charters necessarily threaten those who defend district schools' performance. In so doing, they can undermine political support for district schools, which over time might result in less funding. Furthermore, many advocates for traditional public schools have seen the move toward market-based reforms as a direct challenge to their claim that poor children need additional resources devoted to their education. Explains Richard Leone, president of the Twentieth Century Fund:

> While there is undeniable evidence that highly targeted and very large additions to current educational expenditures would enhance the education of poor children, the political realities of the [times] make such a remedy a nonstarter. Innovations involving organizational and management changes seem especially attractive since, by contrast, they usually are described as involving lower, or even no, increases in spending. Thus, advocates of such ideas as vouchers, choice, privatization, charter schools, and a variety of other current proposals for changes in public education have found an interested audience all across the political spectrum.

Some charter schools simply get by with less. But others . . . turn to private sources for money.

Similarly, some school finance advocates also see charters as a threat to their movement. Over the last 30 years, litigation challenging state and local school financing has been an important mechanism for those who seek to increase funding for low-income schools. Money figures greatly in these lawsuits, because plaintiffs frequently rely on the fact that the allegedly inadequate school districts are funded at a lower level than some of the adequate ones. Of the state courts that have reached the issue, most have ruled that there is reliable evidence that spending is correlated with educational opportunity. Charters and other market reforms could jeopardize this progress, however. As two school finance experts argue, if alternatives outside the traditional public system are premised on the notion that schools do not need more funding to succeed, they "may subvert the goals of the school funding reformers" by reducing "taxpayer incentive to improve public school funding."

The fears of district school supporters are reinforced by some of the rhetoric of school choice proponents. In the battle for public opinion, arguments against spending more on schools are often expressly linked to demands for choice. For example, during the 2004 presidential campaign, [education researchers] Jay Greene and Marcus Winters criticized [Democratic presidential nominee] John Kerry for clinging "to the habitually fruitless path of spending more money," rather than endorsing the "promising reforms of high-stakes testing and school choice." As the state has begun to lose its monopoly over public education, these critics cite the market-oriented reforms as proof of their claim that district schools do not need more money. This is most pronounced in the context of private choice initiatives such as vouchers or tuition tax credits. As researchers from the Heritage Foundation argue, because private schools cost less than district ones, private school choice "may yield billions in savings to states and school districts.". . .

Charters Receive Less Money than Traditional Schools

Charters in fact typically receive fewer public dollars than traditional public schools—on average, nationwide, $1800 less per pupil. In response, some charter schools simply get by with less. But others, including some of the nation's most well-regarded, turn to private sources for money. . . .

For some privatization advocates, the prominence of private philanthropy has its benefits. The traditional market discipline argument for charter schools was that they would have to deliver a high-quality product to compete for students. In one sense, the battle for philanthropic dollars is simply an extension of that rationale, as schools compete to prove their worth to private donors. Moreover, perhaps private donors are better able to identify quality schools than is the public sector. In addition, for those who seek to shrink government's role, even partially shifting the responsibility for education funding from the public to the private sector is a step in the right direction.

While public funding for schools can . . . rise and fall, government funds are generally considered more stable than private contributions.

Is the Reliance on Private Funding Dangerous?

On the other hand, charter schools' reliance on private philanthropy is possibly the Achilles heel of this quasi-market reform. Many current charter operators are gambling on their ability to convince private funders to focus indefinitely on their problem (K-12 education) and solution (charter schools) above others. Education—particularly K-12 schooling for lower-class and minority students—now has the attention of lawmakers, philanthropists, and the American public. As a result, an increasing amount of philanthropic giving is directed there. For example, in 1998 foundations gave $620 million to elementary and secondary schools, and $1.07 billion to higher education. By 2003, giving to higher education had remained flat at $1.12 billion, but giving to K-12 education had doubled to $1.23 billion.

However, no single social issue remains dominant. The environmental movement discovered this in the late 1980's and 1990's, when, after two decades of remarkable growth and sustained individual and foundation giving, interest and money started to move to other causes. In addition, individual foundations change their focus, sometimes moving away completely from sectors that previously had been priorities. This may happen after thoughtful and strategic analysis, or simply because a new director has his own pet project. For the defunded sector and its constituents, the results are the same. This should be a particular concern to the charter school movement, as a majority of giving to school choice–related causes comes from just two foundations—the Bill and Melinda Gates Foundation and the Walton Family Foundations. Together, Gates and Walton gave 6 out of every 10 foundation dollars that went to school choice in 2002.

It is in the self-interest of . . . charter operators to argue for increased funding for district schools.

The role of private philanthropy in funding successful charter schools, therefore, presents another paradox: deregulation has allowed school entrepreneurs to develop creative educational approaches and find alternative funding, yet the deregulated structure ensures the funding rests on uncertain ground. While public funding for schools can also rise and fall, government funds are generally considered more stable than private contributions. And though charter schools are not alone in relying on private philanthropy, schools like KIPP [Knowledge Is Power Program] and some of the others . . . have been uniquely successful at raising enormous sums of money and spending it on schools in high-poverty neighborhoods. As a result, increasing numbers of poor and working class parents see, and are encouraged to see, these schools as their children's best hope for a better life. Yet many of them rest on a partially privatized, precarious financial base....

Charter and Public Schools as Allies

[C]urrently charters are clamoring for equal funding. If they succeed, they will have every incentive to join traditional public school advocates and argue for increased funding for all schools. To see why this is so, consider the case of Chris Whittle, the founder of Edison Schools. Whittle began Edison on the premise that existing government funding for education was sufficiently generous that he could make a profit running schools. After 10 years in the business, he now argues for increased public funding. This is not surprising. More funding will allow him to run better schools, or increase his profits, or both. But given the structure of education financing, in order to achieve his goals, he needs to convince government to allocate greater sums not only to his schools, but to all schools. In other words, it is in the self-interest of Whittle and other charter operators to argue for increased funding for district schools....

Finally, it is worth considering that if charters do become an additional constituency for education, they will be an especially well-placed one. The groups most associated with arguments for increased funding are the unions of teachers and other education professionals. These organizations are seen as an obstacle to reform by many, especially—though not exclusively—those in the Republican Party. Perhaps the most extreme example of the hostility was demonstrated when President [George W.] Bush's former Education Secretary Rod Paige called the National Education Association (NEA) "a terrorist organization." By contrast, Republicans have supported the charter school movement, promoted individual successful schools, and lauded individual charter leaders. Arguments by charter operators that schools need greater funding may resonate with a different constituency than would the same argument coming from the American Federation of Teachers.

4

Charter School Competition Improves the Public Education System

George M. Holmes, Jeff DeSimone, and Nicholas G. Rupp

George M. Holmes is a research fellow in health economics and finance at the University of North Carolina. Jeff DeSimone is assistant professor of economics at the University of South Florida. Nicholas G. Rupp is assistant professor of economics at East Carolina University.

An important question concerning the relationship between charter and traditional public schools is whether the competition between them improves school-wide performance at the traditional public schools. The growth of charter schools in North Carolina and their proximity to traditional schools make North Carolina a good test case for studying the issue. Evidence in North Carolina demonstrates that traditional public schools experience substantial improvements in performance when spurred by competition from charter schools.

Most research on charter schools, and the most intense public debate over their desirability, has focused on the impact of these new schools on the students who attend them. But charter proponents also hope that the threat of students' leaving will spur traditional schools to higher levels of achievement. In the long run, such system-wide improvements, if positive, could even outweigh any negative effects on the individual students they enroll.

Can competition from a new kind of public school, right around the block or down the road in many cases, inspire traditional schools to improve? We address this question here by examining the link between the establishment of charter schools in North Carolina and average student proficiency rates at the traditional public schools most affected by the new source of competition.

Measuring School Improvement

Our use of proficiency rates, an aggregate measure of school performance, distinguishes our work from other recent studies that examine the performance gains made by individual students. However, aggregate school performance is the focus of state accountability systems, is reported in the media, and presumably is used by parents, along with their own observations of their child's progress, to evaluate the quality of their child's school. Schools intent on retaining students can be expected to concentrate their efforts on this indicator.

Ironically, there could be a disjunction between that aggregate and the average performance of individuals at the school, for a variety of reasons. Schools affected by competition could encourage low-performing students not to take the test, could focus their efforts exclusively on students at the cusp of proficiency, or could use any number of strategies to achieve the appearance of improved performance without ensuring that students were actually learning more.

Our results indicate that traditional public schools in North Carolina responded to even the limited competition provided by charter schools by improving their average proficiency rates. However, a comparison of our results with those of other studies that examine the learning gains made by individual students suggests the need for caution in interpreting our results as unambiguously positive.

Using North Carolina Schools as a Test Case

In three short years, from the 1996–97 school year to that of 1999–2000, the final year of our analysis, the number of charter schools in operation in North Carolina rose from zero to 74. By 2004–05, the number had grown to 99; state law currently [as of 2005] caps the total number of charter schools at 100. Because the effects of competition on the performance of traditional public schools can be identified best during periods in which the amount of competition is changing, these years offer a convenient way to test the effects of expanded school choice.

North Carolina provides an unusually stiff test of the theory that charter schools will spur improvement among traditional public schools.

Of course, school choice was not altogether absent in North Carolina even before 1997–98. It was largely limited to choosing to live in a particular district, enrolling a child in a private school, or educating the child at home, all of which require a substantial investment of resources, fiscal or otherwise. Roughly 70 percent of districts also offered parents some degree of choice among public schools or the option of applying to a magnet school. Our results should therefore be interpreted as the effect of the introduction of additional competition from charter schools.

As in most states, students in North Carolina can leave a traditional public school and enroll in a charter, at will and for no monetary cost. Charter schools may not discriminate among students by ability, socioeconomic status, or eligibility for special education. Even so, there are reasons to suspect that the amount of additional competition provided by charter schools is relatively modest. Despite the rapid growth in the number of charter schools in the state, the 12,000 students enrolled in charters in 1999–2000 represented just 1 percent of North Carolina's 1.25 million public-school students. Moreover, before granting a charter, sponsors must consider local impact statements prepared by the district in which the school will be located. Perhaps for this reason, many charter schools in North Carolina target at-risk students and presumably do not pose a competitive threat to traditional public schools. Finally, research conducted by Robert Bifulco and Helen Ladd [in 2005] indicates that North Carolina charter schools during this period may have been less effective in improving student achievement than were traditional public schools, at least for students who attended both charter and traditional public schools between grades 4 and 8. Although it is not clear that parents would have an accurate perception of charter schools' effectiveness, particularly in the early years of the state's program, all these factors, taken together, indicate that North Carolina provides an unusually stiff test of the theory that charter schools will spur improvement among traditional public schools.

Measuring Competition

The North Carolina Department of Public Instruction began testing students at the end of each school year in 1996–97 as part of its ABCs of Public Education program. These tests are taken statewide by all students in grades 3 through 8 in math and reading, and in grades 4 and 7 in writing. We take as our indicator of each school's performance its performance composite for grades 3 through 8, which the state computes as the percentage of tests taken in all three subjects that meet the state's proficiency standard. Since the performance composite is widely reported by the media, schools have strong incentives to improve their rating.

The influence of a nearby charter school on traditional public schools in the area depends, in part, on the credibility of students' threats to switch to the charter [school]. Those threats become more credible as the distance between the schools decreases. Since charter schools charge no tuition, travel costs are the major component of the price of attending one, especially in North Carolina, where charter schools are not required to provide transportation.

These comparisons provide consistent evidence that charter-school competition raises the performance composite of traditional public schools.

We therefore base our measures of the extent of charter competition facing each traditional public school on the school's distance from the nearest charter school. We first map the latitude and longitude of traditional public schools and charter schools throughout the state, identify the charter school closest to each traditional public school, and compute the aerial distance between the two. Then we develop separate indicators for each school of whether there is a charter school within 5 kilometers, 10 kilometers, 15 kilometers, 20 kilometers, and 25 kilometers.

We exclude from the analysis schools, mostly in rural areas, with addresses we were unable to map and schools with missing test performance measures for any year during our study period, which spans 1996–97 to 1999–2000. These exclusions represented about 7 percent of the total. We also drop schools located in three North Carolina Outer Banks counties with substantial water boundaries because straight-line distance is a poor proxy for actual travel time to and from these localities. The analysis includes all of the remaining 1,307 traditional public schools in the state.

The average performance composite among traditional public schools increased from 67 percent in 1996–97 to 75 percent in 1999–2000 as the number of charter schools in the state increased from 0 to more than 70. Meanwhile, after the first charter schools opened in 1997–98, the average distance from a school to the closest charter school fell by about one-third, from 19.2 miles to 12.6 miles in 1999–2000. Is there a connection between these improvements in test-performance scores and growing competition from charter schools?

Expanding the number of charter schools . . . seems like a promising, and far more cost-effective, alternative to lowering class size.

Charter School Competition with Traditional Public Schools

To answer this question we examine whether the annual changes in performance made by traditional public schools during this period were more positive in schools with charter schools nearby than in schools not facing charter school competition. In these comparisons, we take into account changes in the characteristics of the student body, including the percentage of students who are Hispanic, the percent African American, and the percent eligible for the federal free lunch program, as well as changes in the school's student-teacher ratio. We also use information on the school's performance composite two years before the year to correct for measurement error in the school's previous-year performance. Finally, we perform separate comparisons using each of our distance-based indicators of charter-school competition.

These comparisons provide consistent evidence that charter-school competition raises the performance composite of traditional public schools. The effect is statistically significant for four of the seven measures of charter-school competition and falls just short of significance for the other three. In each case, the results indicate that, all else being equal (including the school's score on the performance composite the previous year), the presence of charter-school competition increases traditional school performance by about 1 percent. This represents more than one-half of the average achievement gain of 1.7 percent made by public schools statewide between 1998–99 and 1999–2000 and is, from a policy perspective, nontrivial.

How nontrivial? One indication comes from the information in our results about the gains in performance made by schools where the student-faculty ratio decreased over this same period. In 2002, the North Carolina governor's office proposed a $26 million increase in the state budget to reduce average class size by roughly 1.8 students. Although the relationship between changes in the student-teacher ratio and changes in school performance is not statistically significant, the size of the relationship suggests that the governor's plan would increase scores by roughly 0.36 percentage points. However, our data indicate that opening a charter school would increase public-school test scores by one full point (1.0). Expanding the number of charter schools therefore seems like a promising, and far more cost-effective, alternative to lowering class size. Since state funding follows the student, an increase in the charter-school system requires no increase in spending.

Our results reveal substantial improvements in traditional public-school performance due to the introduction and growth of charter-school choice.

One possible alternative explanation for the improvements observed in traditional public schools when a charter school opened nearby is the migration of lower-performing students from the traditional public school to the charter school. However, simple tests we conducted, based on changes in the average previous-year test scores of students in schools affected and unaffected by charter-school competition, suggest that, if anything, the opposite phenomenon occurred: students switching from traditional public to charter schools appear to have been above-average performers compared with the other students in their school. The fact that traditional public schools experienced net gains in performance, despite a slight decrease in average student quality, suggests that our estimates of the effects of charter-school competition may understate the true effect of charters on traditional public schools.

Results from Other Studies

The findings presented here differ from those of two previous studies that examine the same hypothesis for North Carolina charter schools. The research by Robert Bifulco and Helen Ladd fails to find an effect of charter schools on the effectiveness of traditional public schools, while a similar analysis by one of us conducted in 2003 reported improvements for students in traditional public schools smaller than the ones estimated here. There are several possible explanations for these differences.

Most important, each of the other studies uses student-level data, which we did not have access to when conducting this research. How could schools improve their performance composite scores without a change in the average gains in achievement made by their students? As discussed above, one possibility is that schools affected by competition would target students who score just below the proficiency cutoff. Roughly 3 percent of students in any given year fail by only one point. If a principal were, for example, to entice one-third of such students to gain a single point, the performance composite would increase by a full percentage point, but the average student-level gain would be tiny and could even be offset by losses made by students safely above or below the proficiency cutoff. Our other research indicates that students in schools affected by competition at or near the proficiency cutoff did in fact make the largest gains.

In short, our results reveal substantial improvements in traditional public-school performance due to the introduction and growth of charter-school choice. Read alongside the results of studies based on student-level data, they suggest that even a little bit of competition from charter schools can force schools to appear to be improving, but that policymakers need to take care to ensure that translates into real gains for the average student.

5

Charter Schools Do Not Address the Problems of Public Education

Lisa Swinehart

Lisa Swinehart is a former educator who researches and writes about educational issues.

Members of the Humanist Association (who believe that humans must be responsible for leading ethical lives and contributing to the greater good) should not support the charter school movement for several important reasons. First, student performance at charter schools lags behind that of students in traditional schools. Second, charter schools sustain or increase the stratification of society by isolating students into socioeconomic or racially homogenous groups. Third, charter schools do not provide diverse opinions and a balanced world view for students. Finally, charter schools take money away from traditional public education and threaten the complete restructuring of the American educational system.

In August 2005 the Humanists of Florida Association opened the first Humanist charter school: the Carl Sagan Academy. Although the academy's mission is admirable, the school is simply replicating the ideals inherent in public education. Qualities such as scientific reasoning, critical thinking, and democratic principles should be central to every public school's mission. But the academy, like all charter schools, di-

Lisa Swinehart, "Charter Schools Don't Solve Real Problems," *The Humanist*, vol. 65, no. 5, September–October 2005. Copyright © 2005 the American Humanist Association. Reproduced by permission of the author.

verts attention away from real problems within the American educational system. The Humanist community shouldn't be detracting from the problem at hand by participating in the charter school movement that instead produces poor academic results, perpetuates the stratification of society, advances a parochial educational atmosphere, and reduces public education funding.

Originally designed to swap autonomy for accountability, charter schools were an experiment in deregulation. A distinct feature of charter schools is that they are unrestricted by many public school requirements. The original theory was that a less restricting environment would produce results that surpassed public schools.

However, the claim that increased autonomy leads to enhanced educational outcomes cannot be verified by recent studies [as of late 2005] conducted on national charter school performance. The National Assessment of Educational Progress [NAEP] conducted in 2003 found that charter school students had lower achievement than their public school counterparts "translat[ing] into about a half year of schooling." Test scores remained lower even after the NAEP adjusted for the higher enrollment rate of minority students.

The current state of the charter school system threatens . . . to amplify the socio-economic disparities among students.

Charter Students Perform Below Public Education Trends

A closer examination of charter schools reveals that students are performing below public education trends. Less than satisfactory performance has been linked to the inability of charter schools to attract quality educators. According to the U.S. Government Accountability Office of the Department of Education, where state law permits, charter schools are exempt from requiring teacher certifications. Only 9 percent of public school teachers are working without certification, while 43 percent of charter school teachers aren't certified. Furthermore, as B. Fuller, M. Gawlik, E.K. Gonzales, S. Park, and G. Gibblings point out in their 2003 report "Charter Schools and Inequality: National Disparities in Funding, Teacher Quality, and Student Support," charter school teachers are more likely to have little or no experience in the classroom. Barring of collective bargaining agreements, no contracts, and unsatisfactory pay could be to blame for the disproportionate amount of unaccredited and inexperienced teachers in charter schools.

One of the vital roles of public education is to provide all students with an equal opportunity to succeed. Proponents of charter schools have criticized this aspect of public education, citing substandard schooling in urban areas as an impediment to equality. Charter schools were originally intended to provide lower-income and minority families with an educational choice. However, the current state of the charter school system threatens instead to amplify the socio-economic disparities among students. As research shows, some charter schools are guilty of isolating children in social or ethnic-specific enclaves. Of the African American students who attend charter schools, for example, the authors of the 2003 report find that three-fourths of them are enrolled in 273 schools. Studies also show that in some states Latino students tend to be overrepresented in charter schools and that these schools tend to spring up in lower income areas. This trend can be linked both to state laws that encourage charter schools to serve disadvantaged children and the susceptibility of inner-city schools to forced conversion under the No Child Left Behind Act [passed in 2001, and signed into law in 2002].

Charter Schools Perpetuate Barriers

Rather than providing a competitive educational environment, however, many charter schools serving disadvantaged students perpetuate existing class barriers by hiring uncertified teachers and providing substandard special education services. According to the aforementioned 2003 study, predominantly African American charter schools are more likely to have unaccredited teachers. And though 43 percent of charter school attendees are eligible for lunch subsidies, only 4.5 percent of these schools receive Title I federal funding to support such programs. In addition, individualized learning plans (IEPs), in place for students who qualify for special education, are only being used by 11 percent of charter schools.

Children reared in this kind of environment are likely to arrive at adulthood with a very narrow view of the world.

Moreover, as group-specific charter schools materialize they threaten to create a more polarized society. Many charter schools are based on the concept of group rights—the belief that curriculum should be tailored to a specific ethnic or social group. Some opponents of charter school education maintain that this type of insular learning actually perpetuates the stratification of society. The public education system was prized for uniting students from diverse backgrounds and fusing together our disparate society by passing on shared knowledge and values. When the shared experiences of public education are removed, the resulting society is no longer made up of groups of individuals trying to find common ground but rather of ethnic and social enclaves divided adversarily.

Charter Schools Do Not Provide a Balanced World View

In line with the issue of segregation is the argument that theme charter schools create a parochial learning environment. The school choice system as a whole encourages parents to select schools for their children that further the parents' own beliefs and values. Unlike public education, charter schools are designed to operationalize parental concepts of childrearing by allowing parents to have influence over curriculum. Thus charter schools have become "identity-building institutions" molded to further reflect the specific identity, politics, ideals, and beliefs of the community they serve. It also opens up the possibility that individuals can misuse the system and impress upon a school and students their own particular and perhaps idiosyncratic beliefs.

Charter schools cease to be harmless experiments in government deregulation and become vehicles for large-scale restructuring.

Children reared in this type of environment are likely to arrive at adulthood with a very narrow view of the world. Public education was originally prized for exposing students to diverse individuals and opinions, thus challenging their preconceived notions of reality. However, theme charter schools, organized around a particular idea, fail to expose students to a balanced view of the world. They rather isolate them with like-minded individuals and indoctrinate them in a set of beliefs at a young age, much like organized religion does.

When group-specific charter schools are used as justification for the establishment of socially and ideologically segregated learning environments, the educational system walks a fine line between promoting specialization in an effort to improve education and using specialization as a means to block the views of opposing groups. Thus, by establishing a Humanist charter school and becoming part of this ideologically questionable system, the Humanist community relinquishes its ability to critique those who support charter schools for rival causes. Humanists also surrender their authority in critiquing those parents who wish to use the educational system as a vehicle to instill in children their own beliefs and values.

Charter Schools Divert Resources from Public Education

Beyond these problems, when students transfer out of public schools and into a charter school they take with them the monies earmarked for their education. Each child that transfers to a charter school in this manner is diverting resources away from public education—a move long opposed by Humanists. The defense of this diversion is that it will allow market forces to pressure the public schools to change in order to retain students. But by this argument charter schools aren't simply about choice. Rather, they are about triggering systemic change. When viewed through this lens, charter schools cease to be harmless experiments in government deregulation and become vehicles for large-scale restructuring.

One central argument of several Carl Sagan Academy supporters is that charter schools are the wave of the future and that the Humanist community should utilize this opportunity as a form of activism. But this shouldn't be justification for involvement in a flawed and ideologically questionable educational trend. With the Carl Sagan Academy having opened its doors the Humanist community should examine the public school system and determine if the values inherent in it are worth saving or if a system prized for uniting and educating diverse individuals should be cast aside in favor of charter schools that have been shown to produce poor academic results and stratified learning while creating a restrictive learning environment.

6

Charter Schools Must Be Publicly Regulated

Anne Allen and Dwan Robinson

Ann Allen is an assistant professor at Ohio State University. Dwan Robinson is a PhD candidate at Ohio State University.

Charter schools, particularly those run by private organizations, often do not have adequate public oversight to ensure that the schools are following state law. In addition, many charter schools run by private organizations provide little or no information for the public whose taxes support them. While proponents of charter schools argue that autonomy from public regulation allows these schools to be more innovative, the evidence does not support this claim. Rather, public oversight makes sure that the organizers of charter schools remain true to the educational needs of the public and not narrowly focused on their own programmatic goals.

In a system of autonomous public charter schools, what are the costs of autonomy, and how might those costs be alleviated? These are questions policymakers in Ohio might well consider as the Supreme Court of Ohio deliberates the constitutionality of public charter schools. [The Ohio Supreme Court ruled in October 2006 that privately operated charter schools are constitutional.] Public charter schools are designed to offer choice to public school students, but the governance of these schools often lacks in public oversight and account-

Anne Allen and Dwan Robinson, "Weighing the Public-Private Balance of Charter School Governance," *The Ohio Collaborative Policy Brief*, October 2006, pp. 1–6. Copyright 2006, The Ohio State University. Reproduced by permission.

ability. This lack of public oversight and consequently the absence of information made available to the public may be jeopardizing the potential of public charter schools to provide choice and innovation for the benefit of all students.

The State of Ohio currently funds 294 public charter schools, of which 115 are sponsored by private entities. The Ohio Department of Education once had sponsoring authority for state public charter schools, but in a revision to Ohio's charter law in 2003 that authority was dissolved, leaving private non-profits in control of those 115 charter schools and the state with the responsibility to oversee the authorizers. The remaining 179 charter schools are sponsored by public entities, including public school districts, educational service centers, and one joint vocational school. The state spends about $425 million a year on public charter schools. One issue raised in the pending Supreme Court case against public charter schools is whether these schools, without direct public oversight, can be considered part of the state's common system of public schooling.

Charter Schools and Accountability

Charter school proponents argue that in this case accountability is market-driven. These schools are more accountable than district schools because parents who are not satisfied with the schools will leave, and as a result, the affected district schools will lose money and be forced to close. Proponents also argue that charter school authorities, like district school authorities, are required to administer state tests, must not exclude students from attending, and must not charge tuition. Charter school proponents cite these regulations as evidence that public charter schools function as a part of the state's system of public education.

Opponents argue that charter schools are not publicly accountable because they are allowed to operate without direct public oversight. The schools may be run by private organizations with private boards and are not universally subjected to public authorizers. This lack of public oversight may also lead to a lack of adherence to current law, including reporting regulations and open meeting laws, opponents argue.

There is little to suggest that autonomy has led to the kind of innovation that supports increased achievement.

The Public Is Not Informed

Given that the spectrum of public-private governance for Ohio's charter schools is broad, policymakers are left to consider how private is too private for a public school. Research indicates that when public charter schools are run by private organizations, practices that typically keep the public informed disappear. Instead, practices such as conducting closed school board meetings or not reporting information to the state occur, making it "impossible to conduct" comparisons with other public schools [according to a 2005 Progressive Policy Institute report] and keep the public uninformed about these schools. In fact, a November 2005 opinion poll conducted by the Thomas B. Fordham Foundation indicates that 55 percent of Ohio citizens know very little or nothing about public charter schools. Only 17 percent of citizens report knowing much about these schools. It is fair to ask, in a publicly funded system of education, how can citizens make informed decisions about public charter schools when they know so little about them?

Research also indicates that the lack of oversight for public charter school boards is likely to lead to insular boards that tend to operate in their own self-interests, and consequently, placing program goals over public goals. Charter school boards that do not operate in the public eye may protect themselves against public scrutiny that should lead to a greater responsibility, for addressing such public interests as equity in educational access and opportunity. [Scholars E.B. Fiske and H.F.

Ladd], who [in 2002] conducted research on New Zealand's market-based education system, write: "when equity concerns came into conflict with other policies, it was equity that suffered." Likewise, in an extensive review of Michigan's charter school movement, [researchers] found that charter schools managed by private management companies operated more like private companies than public institutions. Their research indicated that charter boards were often picked and then perpetuated by the private companies managing the school, and the private nature of the companies allowed for the charters to maintain proprietary status over information that in traditional schools is considered public.

[Fifty-three] percent of respondents in a poll oppose or strongly oppose public charter schools being free of many of the rules and regulations traditional school districts face.

Autonomy Does Not Necessarily Lead to Innovation

The idea behind autonomous public schools is one of innovation and experimentation. Autonomy provides freedom from bureaucratic barriers that prevent school leaders and school reformers from making significant change that leads to student achievement. After 10 years of national experimentation with public charter schools, there is little to suggest that autonomy has led to the kind of innovation that supports increased achievement. In fact, the lack of regulation may have created the opposite effect: a system of schooling in which poor performing charters remain open and continue to draw state financing away from district schools.

Rapid Growth Impedes Oversight

Ohio supports one of the fastest growing charter school movements in the nation, which may be cause for concern. The rapid growth of Ohio's charters may have impeded policy-makers from developing an effective system of oversight. Further, it is likely that pressure from private organizations and charter advocacy groups has led to reductions in the kinds of regulations [University of California, San Diego, professor Julian] Betts notes are necessary for "good public policy." The kind of regulations Betts describes aim to create a market that ensures equitable access and information dissemination, including information about achievement rates. "We have consumer protection laws and government oversight in all sorts of markets; the market for schools should not be an exception to this rule."

The majority of Ohioans appear to agree. Recent poll data also show that citizens in Ohio believe public charter schools should follow the same rules and regulations as traditional school districts. Specifically, 53 percent of respondents in a poll by the Fordham Foundation oppose or strongly oppose public charter schools being free of many of the rules and regulations traditional school districts face.

In a market system of public school that is not well-regulated, the true losers are not the schools that are losing money or services ... it is the children in those schools.

Taking time to understand both what is working and what is not working is vital to ensuring a quality system of public charter schools. Also important is increased attention to public oversight of Ohio's public charter schools. In states where more careful attention has been paid to both public oversight and planned growth of charter schools, the charter school movement has proven to be more successful. For example, many of the accomplishments of charter schools authorized by Chicago Public Schools (CPS) have been attributed to the slow growth and methodical planning that has occurred in CPS.

The district has established an office to provide oversight for district charter schools. In addition, the district advertises request for proposals (RFPs) for charter schools, identifies operators to consider submitting RFPs, and communicates desired goals for success and detailed expectations for charter school performance. CPS is highly selective during the application process and approves only 15%–20% of the applicants that respond to the RFPs. The result of this cautious approach is that many Chicago charters are out-performing comparable public school programs.

Without policy protecting the public's interests in these [charter] schools, there is little to prevent the exercise and abuse of private power.

There is no doubt the charter school movement has had some positive effects on public schooling in Ohio. As a result of the pressure from the charter school movement, district schools are beginning to open up their doors to communities in ways that are long overdue. However, sound public policy must be concerned about the effects of the market on all students. In a market system of public schooling that is not well-regulated, the true losers are not the schools that are losing money or services. Instead, it is the children in those schools who, for whatever reason, must remain in schools with reduced resources.

Rigorous Accountability

In order to meet their potential as a public system of choice for all students, public charter schools need more rigorous accountability. Charter school advocates are calling for authorizers to increase their diligence in overseeing charter schools through training for authorizers and more accountability of charter schools by individual school sponsors. Charter advocates also have recognized the need for a better system of information to the public.

What advocates fail to support is increased government regulation of public charter schools. However, if in fact actors on both sides of the charter school debate recognize a need for increased accountability in order to ensure increased quality of these public schools, policy directing a higher level of accountability may well be required. Without policy protecting the public's interests in these schools, there is little to prevent the exercise and abuse of private power. The question the court and other policymakers need to address is what can be done to provide choice in a way that protects the public's interest in fair and equitable education for all students.

The answer is not to do away with choice, but to understand that public charter schools are only quasi-public schools. These schools must continue to operate with public oversight and adhere to regulation in order to ensure that equal and open access is available for all students. Furthermore, by operating in the public eye, charter schools would protect themselves against isolation from public interests. They would also protect the public from a growing ignorance of what these schools are, whom they serve, and how they operate. Information must flow to the public so that the public might be better equipped to make decisions. That is not to say, however, that charter schools should go back to a level of regulation that prevents them from attempting the innovations some set out to design, but Ohio's charter school policy does not come close enough to requiring sufficient public oversight to warrant public status and public funding.

Balancing Autonomy with Public Oversight

The issue policymakers need to consider is how to balance autonomy with responsibility for public interests and public oversight. Here are some possibilities:

- Reverse the decision to allow private sponsorship of public charter schools and create a system of public authorizers to monitor public charter school boards. Authorizers should be close enough to the schools to provide effective oversight but far enough away to allow for autonomy. County-level public authorizers or district boards may provide such a mix. By encouraging closer ties to local public governing bodies, policymakers will be promoting valuable partnerships that support a system of school choice that enhances rather than divides public resources for public education. Through such partnerships, school districts could be looked at as entities offering innovation and diverse educational experiences in the marketplace and charter schools could have greater public legitimacy through a local public authority.

- Establish criteria for charter school boards that include an expectation of diverse representation to protect against these boards serving singular and insular interests.

- Increase access to public meetings and thereby increase opportunities for expression by enforcing laws that oblige all public charter school boards to conduct meetings in open and accessible buildings.

- Require board training for public charter school board members to ensure all board members have at least an initial understanding of their public responsibilities.

- Increase the flow of information to the larger community by requiring that regular reports be published and distributed to the community at large. Increasing information flow between public school academies and local neighborhoods will provide citizens the opportunity to examine what benefits these provide the community and how citizens can contact the school's public authorities for questions or concerns.

The issue of accountability of public charter schools goes well beyond parents entering and exiting a school. Accountability of public education is an issue of protecting public interests. Because charter schools are seen as autonomous institutions of innovation, many may argue that they should be free from the constraints of regulation. However, these quasi-public schools using public dollars have the same responsibility for serving public interests as our district schools. Public oversight that ensures and in fact enforces attention to public interests is a necessary component of all such institutions. Without such oversight, we risk school authorities placing programmatic goals over the more public aims of public education.

7

Regulations on Charter Schools Should Be Reduced

Paul T. Hill

Paul T. Hill is a research professor in the Daniel J. Evans School of Public Affairs and director of the Center on Reinventing Public Education, both at the University of Washington.

In order to be a successful movement, charter schools must grow in numbers and develop distinct curricula. This can only happen, however, if charter schools are not faced with an overabundance of regulations. Opponents of charter schools have worked hard to increase the regulations placed on charters, including legislation that would require charter schools to hire only certified teachers, thereby undermining their chances for success. The health of the movement depends on the removal of caps on the number of charter schools in a state, allowing charters to hire noncertified teachers, and allowing private organizations to obtain charters. Deregulation is essential for charter school success.

Many people who supported charter schools from the beginning did so because of what they could envision developing in the long run. They could imagine a big city like Chicago or Cleveland having an education system very much like the marketplace for independent schools in a wealthy city like San Francisco or Seattle. In a city with a mature charter school sector:

Paul T. Hill, "Realizing Chartering's Full Potential," *Charter Schools Against the Odds*, Cambridge, MA: Hoover Press, 2006. Copyright © 2006 by the Board of Trustees of the Leland Stanford Junior University. Reprinted with the permission of the publisher, Hoover Institution Press.

- Families would have many options and schools' specialties, strengths, and weaknesses would be well known so that parents know what they are choosing; moreover many options would be available to the poor, not just the well off;

- Information would be plentiful about what individual schools do well and badly, and how all schools perform on common outcome measures;

- Except for the newest entrants, all schools would have clear track records so both parents and public oversight bodies can consider long-term outcomes like graduation rates, student performance at the next level of education, college attendance and graduation, and employment success as well as short-term outcomes like test scores;

- Teachers could select the schools that best match their interests, that most need their individual skills, and that are willing and able to pay for classroom excellence;

- New teachers and individuals with rare skills could compete for jobs and be paid for the value of their contribution to the school, not just for their seniority or degrees attained;

- Many teachers and administrators would have experience working in schools of choice and understand the importance of collaboration, sharing responsibility, and paying close attention to parents;

- Organizations that run schools, though varied in their approach to instruction, would all have strong incentives to invest in good instruction and work hard to maintain quality;

- Schools that had bad performance records or lose the confidence of parents will be unable to remain open;

- There would always be room for a school with a powerful new idea—including new uses of time, place, and technology—or a way to meet a previously unmet need;

- Business and financial institutions would understand schools and compete to supply them with everything from loans and insurance to facilities, maintenance, and supplies.

Chartering needs the running room to function as a bona fide demonstration of "different."

The Hope of Charter Schools

[Studies] show that local marketplaces can develop in this way under the right combination of circumstances. No one thought such a situation would emerge overnight. The behemoth of bureaucratic-style public school "systems" was too well entrenched and politically powerful. The alternative would develop gradually, as the first charter schools developed loyal clienteles and attracted more applicants than they could admit, and created a demand for additional charters. As the number of schools grew, so would the number of parents who expected to send their children to charter schools and the numbers of teachers and parents who had charter schools experience and knew how to work effectively within them. Companies and financial institutions, at first unfamiliar with charter schools, would develop lines of business to serve them. School districts, facing competition for students from nimbler and more efficient schools, would seek to compete by devolving important decisions about spending and staffing to the building level and cutting back their central office overhead. Ultimately, all schools would compete on the same basis, and the reinvented district would be as aggressive about pursuing new ideas and seeking replacements for low-performing schools as were the charter schools. Innovations . . . would become widespread, and the whole public education system would always be open to new ideas.

The Charter School Movement Needs Running Room

The situation described above can emerge only if the charter sector grows steadily over time and large numbers of schools develop into well-defined educational options. Today [2006], newness and small scale are themselves barriers to the success of charter schools. Civic and educational leaders who hope chartering will attain the broad vision sketched above need to make sure the movement survives long enough for its schools to develop track records for quality instruction. But a few good schools are not enough. A large-scale alternative can only emerge once people can actually visualize how it would work in practice, not just in theory. Chartering needs the running room to function as a bona fide demonstration of "different."

Proposed legislative changes that would create a bias toward [teacher] unionization . . . could cripple charter schools.

Looked upon from the future, today's charter schools will be seen as pioneers that fought their way uphill and gradually developed a marketplace of real options. Though many good things have happened in the charter school movement, it is still a very long way from realizing this vision. This is true in part because starting good schools and building a track record can't happen overnight; it takes years, more than the charter school movement has had to date. Another and probably more important reason is that opponents of charter schools have understood the long-term vision perfectly and have worked to prevent it by tilting the playing field against charter schools. . . .

Regulations Damage the Charter Movement

The opponents work continually to tilt the playing field even more steeply against charter schools. It is not clear, for example, how much more the movement can grow if state legislatures stick with existing caps on school numbers, or if funding arrangements and government authorizers' duties are not made fairer and more neutral. To date, charter schools have defeated most efforts to unionize their teachers, but proposed legislative changes that would create a bias toward unionization and coverage by district collective bargaining agreements could cripple charter schools. . . .

Caps on the numbers of schools can prevent groups with sound ideas from opening charter schools.

Despite opponents' efforts to tilt the playing field against charter schools, charter schools have many advantages over schools run by politically controlled bureaucracies. These advantages include discretion over use of funds, ability to use time, money, and instructional technologies in innovative ways, freedom to hire teachers and to compete for people of high ability by offering attractive packages of working conditions and pay. They also have access to philanthropic investment and to private risk capital.

However, a profoundly hostile regulatory environment makes it difficult for schools to exploit these advantages. Highly capable organizations are less likely to try providing schools if the field is tilted against them. Because so many obstacles are rooted in public policy, or in the lack of market provision of key goods and services, individual schools cannot overcome them. Overcoming supply side barriers requires concerted action by pro-choice policy activists, philanthropists, businesses, and school heads. . . .

Caps Must Be Eliminated

Caps on the numbers of schools can prevent groups with sound ideas from opening charter schools, and can prevent the charter sector in any locality from gaining the advantages of large scale. This in turn denies families access to a real marketplace of viable options. Fixed limits on charter terms, often three to five years with no clear criteria for renewal, can force charter schools to fight for their lives just as staff and families have learned how to work together effectively. Term limits also put all charter schools, even highly effective ones, at risk of politically motivated non-renewal. Each can discourage some capable entrepreneurs from starting schools.

State laws can limit schools' freedom of action by requiring them to hire only certified teachers . . . [cutting] off . . . access to artists, musicians, and mathematicians and scientists who are not certified teachers.

The same provisions can discourage financial institutions from developing lines of business, lending money to charter schools, insuring them, and providing goods and services that district-run public schools get from their central offices but that charter schools need to buy. . . .

Charter law provisions that bar for-profit firms from receiving charters and groups holding a charter from operating multiple schools also cut off important sources of entrepreneurship and private investment.

Charters Should Be Free to Hire Noncertified Teachers

Finally, state laws can limit schools' freedom of action by requiring them to hire only certified teachers. This can cut off charter schools' access to artists, musicians, and mathematicians and scientists who are not certified teachers. It can also force charter schools to hire teachers in a labor market where wages have been artificially inflated by restrictions on supply, and discourage experimentation with technology-rich instructional methods that require new kinds of teachers. Federal law also interferes with charter schools' access to good teachers, via the NCLB [No Child Left Behind] "highly qualified teacher" requirement. Because this rule has been interpreted to favor education-school-trained teachers, it limits charter schools' ability to make innovative use of artists, scientists, mathematicians, and other masters of key subject matter.

Remedies to Overregulation

Pro-charter people shouldn't kid themselves that the movement can live with these provisions. They are, as intended, strong barriers against the emergence of a healthy charter sector. The remedies are clear enough. Charter laws need to be amended to:

- Empower new authorizers, including colleges and universities, mayors, and qualified nonprofits in states where school boards hold a monopoly on authorizing charter schools.

- Protect charter schools from arbitrary denial of applications by establishing appeal processes, to a state agency or independent body, in each state.

- Eliminate arbitrary caps on the numbers of charter schools. Amend state laws so that the number of charter schools depends only on the availability of competent and willing school providers.

- Eliminate fixed terms for charter schools, in favor of provisions that make it clear a school's charter is valid only as long as it can demonstrate student learning.

- Eliminate bans on for-profit firms holding charters directly, in favor of common funding and oversight provisions for all charter schools, no matter who runs them.

- Allow an organization holding one charter to operate multiple schools as long as all their schools meet agreed performance expectations.

- Allow charter schools to employ teachers and administrators in whatever numbers, and with whatever mixtures of skill and experience necessary to deliver the school's instructional program. All authorizers have ample power to reject a charter proposal in which the staffing plan does not match the instructional methods to be used.

Charter Schools Must Lobby for Change

Charter school associations are pursuing this legislative agenda in a few states, but in most states charter school supporters have no agenda other than defending what little they have. This needs to become a multi-state agenda with designated initiative leaders and agendas in each state.

A model for the kind of multi-state legislative campaign required is the national Business Roundtable's standards-based reform initiative, which the organization pursued in the early 1990s. After creating a common nationwide legislative agenda, the Roundtable designated leadership groups in every state to press governors and key legislators to enact it. The national Roundtable provided materials and assistance to designees in every state, and produced an annual state-by-state progress report. The result was a much more concerted, and ultimately effective, legislative strategy than any one state business group would have pursued on its own.

The national business community has not stepped up on charter schools, preferring less controversial if less effective reforms. However, others can imitate their tactics. A similar foundation-backed effort, managed by the national Alliance of Public Charter Schools, could be effective.

8

Charter Schools and Traditional Public Schools Should Receive Equal Funding

Heather R. Ngoma

Heather R. Ngoma is the director of the New Jersey Charter School Resource Center at Rutgers University's Center for Effective School Practices.

One reason charter schools were started was to address the achievement gap between white students and African American and Latino children. Two New Jersey schools demonstrate how effective charter schools can be in closing the gap. However, charter schools do not receive funding equal to the amount received by district public schools. In addition, the state does not require school districts to provide buildings for charter schools in their districts. Justice requires that charter school students receive the same funding as students at traditional public schools.

Last month [April 2007] the nation embarked on a campaign for justice that resulted in Don Imus being fired from his talk radio show for racist and sexist comments about the Rutgers Women's Basketball team. Shortly after, hip-hop artists were threatened with censorship for their use of inappropriate words when referring to blacks and women.

While Imus's remarks and some hip-hop lyrics are problematic, dealing with these individual incidents of injustice will hardly bring about transformational changes needed in

Heather R. Ngoma, "How Charter Schools Help New Jersey's Children," *The Record*, May 7, 2007, p. L07. Copyright © 2007 North Jersey Media Group, Inc. Reproduced by permission.

our nation. Institutional challenges like educational justice should be our priority. Let us be reminded of this as we nationally recognize charter schools this month.

One of the longest-standing egregious injustices in this nation is that our public schools do not produce the same achievement results for children of all races. Black and Latino children consistently lag behind their white peers on standardized tests, graduation rates and college matriculation rates.

Research suggests that the persistent achievement gap results from a variety of problems, including funding, resources, teacher quality, curriculum, family involvement and expectations. Many states introduced charter schools as a mechanism for addressing these racial-achievement disparities.

Charters are tuition-free public schools operated independently of districts to provide educational options to children. They are not a panacea. However, when operated well, they can be extremely effective, as in the case of Robert Treat Academy Charter School.

The accountability feature inherent in charter schools guards children from education malpractice.

Closing the Achievement Gap

Located in Newark [New Jersey], a city plagued with the many challenges characteristic of any large urban city, the Treat Academy has demonstrated impressive results. The school is 77 percent Latino, 18 percent black and 5 percent white and Asian; 65 percent of the children qualify for free and reduced-price lunches.

In 2005, fourth-graders achieved a 98 percent pass rate for both math and language arts on state-mandated tests. In addition, the school has become a magnet for college preparatory school recruiters looking to lure inner-city students to their schools.

The first graduating class in 2005 received more than $4 million in high school scholarship offers; subsequent classes have achieved similar record amounts.

Robert Treat is not an anomaly. North Star Academy Charter School of Newark is also closing the achievement gap. The high school is 85 percent black, 15 percent Latino, with 90 percent of its students qualifying for free and reduced-priced lunches. In 2005, 100 percent of North Star Academy's 12th-grade general education students achieved proficiency on the New Jersey High School Statewide Assessment (HSPA), exceeding the state average of 85 percent for all New Jersey students.

At 95 percent, North Star's college acceptance and matriculation rate at four-year colleges and universities is the highest of any New Jersey school, including wealthy suburban high schools, with some graduates attending colleges such as Mount Holyoke College, Boston College, Syracuse University, University of Chicago and Rutgers University.

Unlike their district peers, children who attend charter schools are not guaranteed a building for their education.

Admittedly, not all charter schools are doing well. However, the accountability feature inherent in charter schools guards children from education malpractice. Underperforming schools can be closed; consequently, all culpable adults lose their jobs.

Justice for Charter Schools

While charter schools represent a viable option for improving public education, some would prefer that charters did not exist. These detractors would rather see the potential of charter school students compromised like some of their peers in large, ineffective urban systems rather than let them succeed at Robert Treat and North Star. Where is the justice in this?

Many may not realize this, but children who attend Robert Treat and North Star are penalized for wanting a better education. These children receive 10 percent less funding than their district peers for their education. They are also denied access to any Abbott parity funding [a court ruling that urban districts receive equal funding with suburban districts in New Jersey] their resident districts keep their share of this money. Where is the justice in this?

Can we agree that [charter school students] . . . deserve full funding and a building to learn in?

Unlike their district peers, children who attend charter schools are not guaranteed a building for their education. There is no funding for facilities, which means that schools like Robert Treat and North Star have to use money set aside for educating children to pay rent. For the children, this may mean fewer teachers, fewer field trips, or even fewer books. Where is the justice in this?

While the nation continues riding its justice wave, let us not sell our efforts short by focusing on individuals and missing opportunities to address more complex institutional challenges like educational justice for black and Latino children.

Justice Demands Equal Funding for Charter Schools

Can we accelerate the growth of more high-performing charter schools while underperforming district schools try to improve? Can we agree to not penalize the children for wanting a good education and a better chance in life? Can we agree that they, too, deserve full funding and a building to learn in?

If we can agree that educational justice will pay far greater dividends for our nation than firing Don Imus or censoring hip-hop artists ever will, then we are on our way to engaging in the transformational work that will advance our nation. Until then, our progress towards justice will be minimal.

9

Charter and Public Schools Should Not Receive Equal Funding

F. Howard Nelson, Edward Muir, and Rachel Drown

F. Howard Nelson, Edward Muir, and Rachel Drown are researchers who work for the American Federation of Teachers Research and Information Services.

Charter schools proponents believe that charter schools do not receive a fair share of public school funding. Although it is true that charter schools do not generally receive the same funding as traditional schools, charter schools are not required to offer the same range of services, including special education and English as a second language courses. In addition, charter schools spend less on food, transportation, and teachers because of fewer regulations. They also receive more funding from private and federal sources than do traditional public schools. For these reasons, they should not receive state funding equal to traditional public schools.

Charter schools have become the nation's most expensive experiment in public school choice, costing roughly $5.2 billion in 2002–03. Surveys of charter school operators continue to show that they believe their biggest problems relate to finances: lack of start-up funds, inadequate operating funds and inadequate facilities. Since few of these surveys include a comparison to regular public schools, however, it is not clear that these perceived financial problems are unique to charter schools. Further, charter school operators may have only a vague idea of how their school's funding is determined or even how much funding they receive.

Just like other public schools, charter schools are expected to file budget reports and financial statements. Though details of charter school financial reporting and compliance are less than perfect, they still allow for a more objective study of charter school financial issues. The National Charter School Finance Study, funded by the U.S. Department of Education, used these records to go beyond superficial revenue and expenditure comparisons to address more precise questions such as: (1) How and why does charter school funding differ from school district funding? (2) Do charter schools get more or less funding than other public schools that offer comparable services for similar students? (3) Are charter school funding systems responsible for differences between charter schools and their host school districts in the way they spend money?

Every school district ... pays for programs for the hearing impaired, private schools for the severely handicapped, and vocational education and other expensive programs.

Charter Schools Receive Their Fair Share

This 12-state study, "Paying for the Vision: Charter School Revenue and Expenditures," found that charter schools in most states usually obtained their fair share of operating funds and frequently their fair share of capital funding. The commonly observed per-pupil revenue difference between charter schools and school districts is partly attributable to the broader mission of school districts (e.g., adult education, infant and toddler special education programs, transportation provided for private school students).

But issues of scale underlie much of the financial pinch felt by charter schools. Small size inevitably elevates per-pupil administration costs, which contributes to less per-pupil spending on instruction. This leads to class sizes differing little from regular public schools, the hiring of lower-paid, inexperienced teachers and high staff turnover rates. Small size makes it nearly impossible for charter schools to offer a full range of special education services. Even the concentration of charter schools in central cities, where schools can rely on parent-provided transportation and school-sized facilities are more readily obtained, can be attributed in part to issues of scale. . . .

The Facts About Charter School Funding

Built on a set of rules and practices conceived to fund regular public schools, charter school funding varies widely across states, possibly determined by school size, the types of students enrolled and the services offered to students. A few atypical charter schools obtain funding well in excess of $20,000 per pupil or more. Most charter schools obtain far less revenue than these atypical schools, in part because they do not enroll very many students in expensive educational programs. Every school district, on the other hand, pays for programs for the hearing impaired, private schools for the severely handicapped, and vocational education and other expensive programs.

Host school districts . . . take on greater financial responsibilities for student support services such as food service and transportation.

---

1. *Charter schools operate with less revenue per student than host school districts.* After looking at all funds (general, special revenue, federal programs, capital outlay, etc.), only District of Columbia charter schools obtained more revenue per pupil than their host school districts. In the other 11 states, charter

schools secured less revenue than their host school districts, ranging from $220 per pupil less in North Carolina to $1,841 per pupil less in Connecticut. This simple comparison of total revenue does not account for the different mix of students and services in school districts compared to charter schools, so it is not a good measure of funding fairness.

2. *Negotiations between school districts and charter schools play a major role in funding.* Charter school revenue estimates in our study incorporate estimates for services and facilities provided by school districts without charge except for special education in California, Colorado and Connecticut. Fair comparisons between charter schools and school districts should account for services (e.g., oversight, transportation, special education services or personnel services) or facilities provided in kind by school districts. The value of in-kind support for facilities and special education was especially important in California and Colorado. School districts in other states may also be required to provide special education (e.g., Connecticut), transportation (e.g., Connecticut, Massachusetts and Pennsylvania) or other services at no cost to charter schools.

3. *School districts have broader and more diverse educational missions than charter schools.* Schools are required to provide special education preschool programs, transportation for private schools, community outreach, adult education and other activities—even paying for charter schools—that are usually not provided by charter schools. These non-core expenditures inflate school district spending, possibly resulting in unfair comparisons with charter schools. Host school districts also take on greater financial responsibilities for student support services such as food service and transportation, which together accounted for about $400 per pupil of the charter school/host school district spending differential.

4. *Charter schools enrolled fewer and less costly special education students than host school districts.* With the exception of

the District of Columbia, host school districts in every state in our study enrolled a higher percentage of special education students than charter schools did, especially students with the most costly disabilities.

The difference in spending on special education between charter schools and school districts is greater than would be predicted when looking at enrollment differences, in part because charter schools are less likely to enroll students with high-cost disabilities. Consequently, special education expenditures per special education student can be several thousand dollars higher in school districts than in charter schools. . . . (School districts in California, Colorado and Connecticut frequently provided special education services for charter schools, so the cost of the services was not in charter school financial records.)

Those expenditures account for much of the total per-pupil spending (for all students, not just special education students) differential between host school districts and charter schools: $313 per pupil in Arizona, $537 per pupil in Michigan, $465 per pupil in Minnesota, $325 per pupil in North Carolina and $497 per pupil in Texas.

5. *Charter schools often served a smaller percentage of low-income and limited-English proficient (LEP) students than host school districts.* Programs for low-income students are also costly. In general, charter school student populations were similar to statewide averages; but compared to host school districts, charter schools in eight of the 12 states in our study enrolled a smaller percentage of low-income students. Arizona, Connecticut, Minnesota and North Carolina charter schools enrolled about the same low-income student population as their host school districts.

Regular public schools were also more likely than charter schools to serve limited-English proficient students. Matched LEP data for charter schools and host school districts existed in eight of the 12 states; charter schools averaged a smaller proportion of LEP students than host school districts in seven. In the U.S. Department of Education's Schools and Staffing Survey (SASS), charter school teachers reported that 8.5 percent of their students were LEP students compared to 13.1 percent of teachers in regular public schools.

Charter schools employed two to four times as many administrators per 100 students than host school districts.

---

6. *Grade level of students served by charter schools was unrelated to funding.* Other research generally indicates that high schools cost more to operate than middle and elementary schools. Our study, however, does not reveal that states providing extra funding for charter high school students had more charter high schools than states not providing the extra funding.

Charter School Spending

1. *Charter schools were small.* Except for a few schools, primarily those managed by private companies, charter schools enrolled fewer students than regular public schools. While the average public school in the United States enrolled about 500 students (and around 700 students in the 100 largest cities), charter school size ranged from an average of fewer than 100 students in Connecticut and Florida to 440 students in California. Though touted as an effective educational strategy, small scale contributes to many of the financial differences between charter schools and district schools, such as high administration costs, difficulty providing special education services, the commonly found absence of student transportation services and school lunch programs, and the pattern of hiring less costly, therefore, less experienced teachers, who leave charter schools at high rates.

2. *Charter schools were concentrated in central cities.* Charter school operators often locate their schools in or near inner

cities, where public schools in general are under scrutiny. But greater population density also offers opportunities to compensate for small scale. The SASS data reveal that 47.3 percent of charter school teachers worked in central cities compared to only 26.9 percent of regular public school teachers. Population density in urban areas allows charter schools to grow larger because student transportation presents fewer problems and facilities of sufficient size to house a charter school may be easier to find.

3. *Charter schools spend more on administration than do host school districts.* While expected to perform the administrative functions of both schools and school districts, charter schools are smaller than other public schools and much smaller than school districts, inevitably resulting in greater per-pupil administrative overhead.

Charter schools employed two to four times as many administrators per 100 students than host school districts (this comparison combines both school and district administrators). Per-pupil expenditures for administration exceeded comparable host school district figures in every state with available data on administrative spending, ranging from $200 to $800 per pupil more in charter schools than school districts.

Charter schools frequently provided no transportation, instead relying on parents of students.

---

4. *Charter schools spend less on instruction than host school districts.* Perhaps because charter schools spend more on administration and, in some states, often need to use operating funds to pay for facilities, they direct fewer resources to classrooms. In every state in our study where expenditures were studied, charter schools spent fewer dollars per pupil on instruction (including special education instruction and other forms of instructional support, primarily library and media)

than host school districts. The differential reached more than $1,000 per pupil in Michigan, Minnesota and North Carolina.

5. *Class size and the pupil-to-teacher ratio were about the same in charter schools and host school districts.* Charter schools are widely believed to emphasize smaller class size, but low spending on instruction makes it difficult to keep class size down. Charter school pupil-to-teacher ratios generally matched or exceeded host school district ratios—by as many as six students per teacher more in Texas and California.

6. *Teacher pay is lower in charter schools than in regular public schools, and teacher turnover is higher.* Less spending on instruction is also reflected in charter schools employing less costly staff. According to the 1999–2000 SASS, charter school teachers are younger, inexperienced and had less formal education compared to teachers in other public schools; 41 percent of charter school teachers had total yearly earnings under $30,000 (compared to 20 percent in regular public schools). Research suggests that teachers choose charter schools for reasons such as working with like-minded colleagues in innovative educational settings, but it is difficult to create this environment when, according to SASS, teacher turnover exceeds 35 percent (compared to about 15 percent in regular public schools).

7. *Charter schools spent less on student transportation than host school districts.* The large geographical area from which charter schools draw students leads to increased transportation costs relative to a system of neighborhood schools. Most states in our study either granted charter schools transportation funding comparable to school district funding or mandated that school districts provide transportation to charter schools, at no cost, from district funds (e.g., Connecticut, Massachusetts and Pennsylvania). Because costs exceed state transportation support by a wide margin, charter schools frequently provided no transportation, instead relying on parents of students. At least two-thirds of the charter schools in Colo-

rado, Michigan, Minnesota, North Carolina and Texas did not report any student transportation costs.

8. *Charter schools spent less on food service than host school districts.* Charter schools may not have the economies of scale needed to operate small categorical aid programs, such as those that support food service, which require the filing of applications and detailed reporting. Financed by meal charges and government funding, especially for poor children, school districts seldom use general operating funds for food service. Our study found that many charter schools provided no food service programs, and those that did often used general operating funds. Charter schools spent an average of $100 per pupil to $200 per pupil less on food service than host school districts. (This average is reduced because it takes into account charter schools that do not provide food service.)

Charter schools obtained significantly more private funding than host school districts.

The Cost of Facilities

Unlike operating revenue, facilities cannot be divided into small pieces that follow children to charter schools or from one charter school to another. From one perspective, facilities for charter schools represent unnecessary new capital costs in states and school districts that have excess classroom space, in part explaining the reluctance of legislatures to fund charter school facilities. Few individual schools lose enough students to charter schools to warrant cutbacks in staff or resources or the closing of schools. Thus, regular public schools spend about the same amount of money to educate fewer students. In the fastest growing states and school districts, however, the presence of charter schools helps avoid at least some new school construction.

The combined per-pupil costs of capital outlay, rent, leases, utilities, cleaning, maintenance, furnishings, equipment such as computers, and technology infrastructure (in the eight states with data) were about the same for charter schools and host school districts, except in fast-growing Colorado and Florida where school districts spent heavily on new facilities. . . .

Private Contributions and Federal Funding Are Greater in Charter Schools

Although charter schools frequently obtained less operating and capital funding from state sources than host school districts received, private funding (an inconsequential source of revenue for school districts) and federal funding helped make up the difference.

1. *Charter schools obtained significantly more private funding than host school districts.*

- Charter schools in the District of Columbia obtained the highest average amount of private funding ($780 per pupil).

- North Carolina and Pennsylvania charter schools averaged the lowest amount of private contributions (about $150 per pupil).

- California and Florida were the most dependent on private funding, as a percentage of total revenue, averaging in excess of 7 percent of total revenue.

- Nontax sources of revenue in Arizona's multisite, for-profit charter schools totaled just $123 per student, compared to $459 per pupil in nonprofit schools.

- Company-run charter schools in Minnesota obtained nontax revenue of $244 per pupil, nearly half of the $445 per-pupil average for other charter schools.

2. *In some states, charter schools obtain more federal revenue than host school districts.* Revenue from the federal govern-

ment represented a larger share of total revenue for charter schools than host school districts in eight of the 12 states—as much as 17 percent of total revenue in Connecticut, the District of Columbia and Florida. Federal charter school start-up funding accounts for all of the difference between charter schools and host school districts in federal funding. In the 1990s, charter schools were sometimes unable to qualify for Title I and special education funding during their first year of operation, but federal legislation enacted in 1998 rectified most of these problems. . . .

Charters Are Too Expensive, Not Underfunded

Sometimes the lackluster academic performance of charter schools is portrayed as an accomplishment because advocates assert that charter schools get less funding and cannot pay their teachers as much money as regular public schools do. A complete examination of financial records, however, offers another way to look at revenue differences: School districts have more expansive educational obligations than the narrower missions pursued by charter schools. School districts provide special education preschool programs, private school services, community outreach, adult education and other activities not usually expected of charter schools. Charter schools also enrolled fewer special education students, especially those with the most costly disabilities. School districts in which charter schools are located tend to serve more low-income and limited-English proficient students in addition to providing more student support services such as transportation and food service. While expected to perform the administrative functions of both schools and school districts, charter schools are smaller than other public schools—and much smaller than school districts. The obvious result is greater per-pupil administrative overhead, contributing to less per-pupil spending on instruction, increased class size, lower-paid, inexperienced teachers and high staff turnover rates.

10

Student Achievement Is Greater in Charter Schools

Caroline M. Hoxby

Caroline M. Hoxby is an economics professor at Harvard University and a researcher at the National Bureau of Economic Research.

A comparison of fourth graders enrolled in charter schools with fourth graders at nearby traditional public schools shows that charter school students are 4 to 5 percent more proficient in reading and 2 to 3 percent more proficient in mathematics than the students at the traditional public schools. There are some exceptions to this finding, and some places where the differences between the two groups of students is too small to be statistically significant. The results of the study suggest that charter school students benefit from their educational experience.

Charter schools are a form of school choice that a growing number of people find interesting. This is because charter schools may provide positive competition for regular public schools. They may also be innovators in school management, curriculum, and the use of technology. They may provide alternatives for children who would otherwise be confined to failing schools. An effective, safe alternative school may be especially important for families who are disadvantaged because they often lack the means to escape a failing school by moving

Caroline M. Hoxby, *A Straightforward Comparison of Charter Schools and Regular Public Schools in the United States,* Cambridge, MA: National Bureau of Economic Research, 2004. http://post.economics.harvard.edu/faculty/hoxby/papers/charters_040909.pdf. Reproduced by permission of the publisher of the publisher and the author.

to another area. Charter schools are public schools and thus accept all students equally. Also, charter schools participate in their states' accountability systems and obey many state and federal regulations. The essential difference between charter schools and regular public schools is that charter schools exist on a fee-per-student basis. If they can attract students, they can grow. However, if they fail to attract students, they will inevitably close. In short, charter schools combine elements of regular public schools and private schools and therefore interest people who want to see reform in American education but who worry about a laissez faire market for education.

A Fledgling Reform

Charter schools are a fledgling reform: they enroll only 1.5 percent of American students. Several states have no charter schools at all, and only 7 states and the District of Columbia have more than 2 percent of their students in charter schools. Thus, charter schools are an important part of federal and state efforts to improve schools mainly because they help policy makers envision the future, not because they already enroll many students. Not surprisingly, much of the public is unfamiliar with charter schools and wonders how students fare in them. This study attempts to fill that gap by providing a comprehensive look at charter schools in the United States. It examines the achievement of 99 percent of fourth graders who attend charter schools. Their performance is compared to that of students in the regular public school nearest them— that is, the school that the charter students would otherwise most likely have attended.

It should [be] said at the outset that this study is useful because it is comprehensive and timely. The comparison it makes is reasonable and helps policy makers answer the question, "What if charter schools did not exist?" However, the best and most scientific way to determine how charter schools affect students is a randomized study that follows students over multiple years. Because charter schools often have more applicants than spaces and are not allowed to select their students, they hold random lotteries among applicants. Therefore, a researcher can compare students who randomly were assigned to enroll and not enroll in a charter school. A researcher can follow the charter school students and the randomly selected comparison group over several years of education, confident that both groups had families who were motivated to apply to charter schools. (Parents may be motivated to apply because they are ambitious for their children, but parents may also be motivated to apply because their children are already performing poorly in their regular school.) In addition, a researcher can often see how students were performing *before* they applied to charter schools. Using preapplication data, a researcher can verify that the lottery was random and show which types of students are attracted to charter schools. . . .

A poorly designed study of charter schools compares apples to oranges—that is, it compares charter schools to schools that the charter students were unlikely to attend.

Comparing Apples to Apples

The reason that randomized studies are so valuable is that they guarantee that a researcher is comparing apples to apples. A randomized study tells us what would have happened to students if they had not attended charter schools. This is the best answer to policy makers' "what if" question: what if charter schools did not exist and students attended whatever school they would have attended in their absence?

A poorly designed study of charter schools compares apples to oranges—that is, it compares charter schools to schools that the charter students were unlikely to attend in any case. Keep in mind that the typical American student does not attend a charter school. Affluent parents whose children are doing fine in suburban schools rarely send them to fledgling charter schools. Instead, charter schools disproportionately arise where families are relatively poor, likely to be racial minorities, likely to speak English as a second language, and likely to have a single parent. Policy makers' "what if" question cannot be answered by, say, comparing a charter school student who would otherwise have attended an inner-city public school to a student in an affluent, suburban school.

[Charter students] are 4.9 percent more likely to be proficient when compared to students in the nearest public school with a similar racial composition.

The American Federation of Teachers (AFT) has recently promoted statistics based on the comparison of fourth graders in charter schools to the typical fourth graders in regular public schools. Much attention has been paid to this crude comparison, and many people have incorrectly interpreted it as sound evidence that charter schools reduce achievement. Little attention has been given to the fact that when the AFT compared black students to black students or Hispanic students to Hispanic students, the results did not confirm the crude comparison. In other words, even a mild attempt to compare apples to apples showed that the crude comparison was misleading. Moreover, the AFT study was based on a sample of only 3 percent of students. Because charter schools enroll only 1.5 percent of students in America, a 3 percent sample amounts to only 4 fourth graders in Connecticut charter schools, 14 in DC [District of Columbia] charter schools, 32 in New York charter schools, and 38 in New Jersey charter schools. Even in the charter-friendly state of Arizona, the number is only 108. A state's charter school policy cannot be evaluated using the equivalent of one or two classrooms of students. An analysis of charter schools that is statistically meaningful requires larger numbers of students.

The Value of a Comprehensive Study

Fortunately, a comprehensive study is possible because charter school students take their states' exams, under the same regulations as apply to students in regular public schools. This study uses assessment data on 99 percent of fourth graders enrolled in charter schools, except that fifth or third graders are used in states that do not test fourth graders. It is important to understand that this is not a sample: it is all charter students for whom results are reported. (The missing 1 percent are in first year start-up schools or schools so small that scores are kept confidential to protect individual students.) Moreover, the comprehensive data make it possible to compare charter schools to the schools that their students would otherwise most likely attend: the nearest regular public school and the nearest regular public school with a similar racial composition. The data make it possible to stay within the neighborhood—a charter school never ends up being compared to regular public schools that are in different states or face very different local circumstances. . . .

The earlier the grade, the more reading results are the precise indicator of school effectiveness.

Results of the Comparison

For the United States as a whole, charter school students are 3.8 percent more likely to be proficient on their state's reading examination when compared to students in the nearest public school. They are 4.9 percent more likely to be proficient when compared to students in the nearest public school with a similar racial composition. These findings are an average over states where charter schools are prevalent and well-established and states that have only a handful of students in fledgling charter schools.

The states where charter schools are relatively prevalent tend to have results that are statistically significant at the state level. . . . Compared to students in the nearest regular public school with a similar racial composition, Alaska's charter students are about 20 percent more likely to be proficient in reading; Arizona's, California's, Massachusetts', and Pennsylvania's are about 8 percent more likely to be proficient; Colorado's, New Jersey's, and Nevada's are 10 to 11 percent more likely to be proficient; Florida's and Georgia's are 5 to 6 percent more likely to be proficient; Hawaii's, Illinois', and Oregon's are 14 to 16 percent more likely to be proficient; and Louisiana's and the District of Columbia's are more than 30 percent more likely to be proficient. North Carolina's charter students are about 4 percent less likely to be proficient in reading. Michigan presents a mixed picture. The results for the nearest public school suggest that charter students are about 4 percent less likely to be proficient in reading, but this result disappears when the comparison group is students in the nearest public school with a similar racial composition. The Michigan results are so sensitive to a small difference in how race is treated that they suggest that student achievement varies significantly by race in Michigan. In consequence, we need to be more careful, not less careful, about comparing charter schools to the schools their students would otherwise likely attend. . . .

For the United States as a whole, charter school students are 1.6 percent more likely to be proficient on their state's math examination when compared to students in the nearest public school. They are 2.8 percent more likely to be proficient when compared to students in the nearest public school with a similar racial composition. It is not surprising that the differences are smaller in mathematics than in reading, simply because schools tend to emphasize the reading skills in the grades leading up to grade four. Thus, the earlier the grade, the more reading results are the precise indicator of school effectiveness. (This tendency reverses itself in secondary school grades, where math results are often more precise measures of achievement.)...

Compared to students in the nearest regular public school with a similar racial composition, Alaska's charter students are about 17 percent more likely to be proficient in math; Arizona's, Massachusetts', and Wisconsin's are about 7 to 8 percent more likely to be proficient; California's are about 3 percent more likely to be proficient; Colorado's and Hawaii's are 12 to 13 percent more likely to be proficient; Illinois' are about 21 more likely to be proficient; Louisiana's are about 29 percent more likely to be proficient, and the District of Columbia's are about 41 percent more likely to be proficient.

On the whole, the results suggest that the average charter school student in the United States benefits from having a charter school alternative.

Exceptions in the Findings

North Carolina's charter students are about 4 percent less likely to be proficient in math. This makes it the only state with both reading and math results that suggest charter school students being at a disadvantage. Texas' charter schools are about 8 percent less likely to be proficient in math. New York and Ohio present mixed pictures because the results for the nearest public school suggest that charter students are about 9 to 10 percent less likely to be proficient in reading, but this result disappears when the comparison group is students in the nearest public school with a similar racial composition. The sensitivity of these results to small differences in how race is treated suggests that achievement varies substantially with race in these states. This should make us more careful about comparing charter schools to the schools from which they actually draw....

Charter School Students Benefit

In this study, charter school students' achievement is compared in a straightforward way to the achievement of students in the nearby regular public schools that the charter students would likely otherwise attend. The results are comprehensive and representative for charter school students in about the fourth grade. Over the United States as a whole, the charter school students are 4 to 5 percent more proficient in reading and 2 to 3 percent more proficient in math. States where charter schools are prevalent tend to have larger positive results, but there are exceptions such as North Carolina. Because there are a number of states with results that are not statistically meaningful or easily interpretable, it is evident that it is early days for evaluating charter schools. On the whole, the results suggest that the average charter school student in the United States benefits from having a charter school alternative. These results should presumably make us patient enough to wait for the results of multi-year studies based on random lotteries among charter school applicants. Such studies use the scientific method most likely to inform policy debates on charter schools.

11

Student Achievement Is Not Greater in Charter Schools

Joydeep Roy and Lawrence Mishel

Joydeep Roy and Lawrence Mishel are researchers at the Economic Policy Institute.

A study conducted by Harvard professor Caroline Hoxby seems to demonstrate that charter school students outperform students at regular public schools. However, a reanalysis of the data suggests that Hoxby did not adequately take into account the racial and economic backgrounds of the students she studied. When charter school students are matched with public school students from a similar racial and/or economic background, the apparent higher achievement by charter school students disappears.

In late summer of 2004 researchers at the American Federation of Teachers (AFT), drawing upon data in a not-yet-published study of charter schools by the National Assessment of Educational Progress (NAEP), issued a report concluding that charter school students had lower achievement in both reading and mathematics compared to students in regular public schools. The differences were significant overall as well as for some of the very groups of students for whom charter schools are said by proponents to offer particular benefits, e.g., low-income children eligible for free or reduced-price lunches and students in central cities. However, the AFT also found that minorities in charter schools had test scores that were not significantly different than those of their counterparts in regular public schools.

A Spirited Debate
Over Student Achievement

The AFT study, reported on the front page of the *New York Times*, generated a spirited debate among researchers and policy analysts in the education community and beyond. In an important rebuttal, Professor Caroline Hoxby of Harvard University argued that the AFT report was fundamentally flawed because of its reliance on the NAEP's small and uneven sample size. In her own study, Hoxby compared reading and math scores of fourth-grade students in nearly all (99%) charter schools to the scores of fourth-grade students in neighboring regular public schools. (She selected fourth grade for consistency with the NAEP sample.) For the country as a whole, Hoxby found that charter school students were 3.8% more likely to be proficient on their state's reading exam when compared to students in the nearest regular public school; the advantage rose to 4.9% when the racial composition of the charter school and the nearest regular public school was similar. The corresponding charter advantages in math were 1.6% and 2.8%. North Carolina was the only state in which charter students' proficiency was lower in a statistically significant way.

Charter schools serve a disproportionately lower share of minorities and low-income students compared to their matched regular public schools.

The Importance of Student Background

Hoxby's analysis, however, suffers from the fact that *her method of comparing charter schools to their neighboring regular public schools (and to those neighboring public schools with a similar racial composition) inadequately controls for student back-grounds.* In her sample of matched schools there are often significant differences in the demographic and socioeconomic characteristics of the students. For instance, comparing the charter schools in Hoxby's sample to the matched neighboring public schools with a similar racial composition shows that the charter schools have a disproportionately higher black population (34% vs. 28%) and higher white population (43% vs. 36%), while the share of Hispanics is lower (18% vs. 30%). Her sample of charter schools also has disproportionately fewer low-income students than does the matched "racially similar" sample of neighboring public schools (49% vs. 60%). The same picture emerges in terms of the demographics of charter schools in central cities: charter schools serve a disproportionately lower share of minorities and low-income students compared to their matched regular public schools. Thus, without further controls, Hoxby's method of comparing "racially matched" schools does not appear to be effective in controlling for student characteristics.

In the four states where charter school students are relatively similar . . . to their peers in matched regular public schools . . . the effect of charter schools is mostly negative in both reading and math.

Hoxby's result of a positive charter effect on math proficiency disappears when racial composition is controlled for directly. Further, when both racial composition and low-income status are controlled for, the positive effect of attending a charter school disappears for both math and reading (it becomes very small and not statistically significantly different than zero). Thus, Hoxby's conclusion that "although it is too early to draw sweeping conclusions, the initial indications are that the average student attending a charter school has higher achievement than he or she otherwise would" does not hold up against direct controls for student background.

Though Hoxby's sample includes charter schools from 37 states, only nine states have close to or more than 50 charter schools. These nine states are considered "major charter states"—the performance of charter schools in these states is of particular interest to policy makers. The states are California (200 schools), Michigan (133), Florida (98), Arizona (96), Texas (90), Ohio (67), North Carolina (65), Colorado (64), and Pennsylvania (48).

Analyses by location show no significant positive impact in either math or reading for charter schools in any type of location: central city, suburb, town, or rural area.

Only California Charters Show an Advantage

Controlling for racial composition, California alone among the major charter states retains a significant charter advantage in reading proficiency. For math, charter schools in none of the nine states have any statistically significant edge over their matched regular public schools. Controlling for low-income status (proxied by free and reduced-price lunch eligibility) in addition to racial composition, only one state (California) has a significant charter school advantage in reading and none in math. In fact, in the four states where charter school students are relatively similar in socioeconomic composition to their peers in matched regular public schools—Michigan, North Carolina, Ohio, and Texas—the effect of charter schools is mostly negative in both reading and math, though the difference is rarely statistically significant.

In terms of solely central city schools, charters have no significant effect in math once racial composition is controlled for: further controlling for low-income status lowers the charter school coefficient. There is a modest and marginally significant positive effect in reading when only racial composition is controlled for, but this advantage vanishes when a control is added for low-income status. In fact, analyses by location show no significant positive impact in either math or reading for charter schools in any type of location: central city, suburb, town, or rural area.

The selective nature of charter schools (students choose to attend charter schools; they are not assigned randomly) may be one reason why some of the smaller states in terms of charter presence enjoy a large charter advantage in Hoxby's results. For example, in Louisiana charter schools outperform their matched regular public schools by 30 points in both reading and mathematics. Yet Louisiana's charter schools are majority white, while the share of whites in the matched public schools is only 12%; there is also a large 40 percentage-point difference in the share of students eligible for free or reduced-price lunches. The case of Nevada is similar: the proportion of whites in charter schools and matched regular public schools is 55% and 26%, respectively, and there is a 30 percentage-point difference in the shares eligible for lunch subsidies.

During the recent controversy generated by the release of the NAEP charter school pilot study results, many education analysts correctly noted that it is problematic to discern the true effect of charter schools on achievement using cross-sectional or "point-in-time" data. Indeed, the most persuasive and informative assessments of charter school performance are based on analyses of longitudinal data (following schools or students over time) that can control for observed and unobserved characteristics of students and schools, especially initial test scores. Nevertheless, cross-sectional analysis has frequently been employed to learn about factors driving educational achievement, including charter schools effects, but they are more persuasive when they control for student and school characteristics. The cross-sectional analyses offered by Hoxby have been widely cited by charter school advocates, including former Secretary of Education Rod Paige. The purpose of this reanalysis is to assess whether Hoxby's cross-sectional matched schools study is useful or informative regarding the impact of charter schools on achievement. . . .

Charter School Advantage Disappears

For the nation as a whole, Hoxby's estimates show charter schools to have a statistically significant 4.9-point advantage in reading proficiency. However, when the racial composition and low-income status at the matched schools are taken into account, the charter school advantage drops sharply. Race alone reduces the charter advantage at the national level to less than a third (from 4.80 to 1.47); the further inclusion of free lunch eligibility drops it to a statistically insignificant 1.10.

As with the national results, the findings of a charter school advantage in most states disappear once direct controls are added for student race and income. In California, the charter school advantage drops by more than half when controlling either for race or for race and poverty, then increases slightly when further controlling for income (note though that data on free lunch eligibility are missing for a large percentage of California charter schools). In three other big states—Arizona, Florida, and Texas—controlling for race and poverty measures yields a negative charter school effect, though the results are generally not significant. In Michigan, the only other state with more than 100 charter schools in the sample, allowing for race and poverty increases the estimated advantage of the charter schools, but it still remains negative. The charter school advantage also drops in major charter states like Colorado (declining from a statistically significant 11-point advantage to a statistically insignificant 1 point) and Pennsylvania (from 8.5 points to less than 1 point). Hawaii, which is not a big charter school state, nevertheless witnesses a huge drop in the charter advantage when controlling for student characteristics.

These differences when race and income are controlled for would seem to suggest that much of the estimated charter school advantage in the Hoxby study reflects the fact that charters tend to enroll students from higher-scoring racial and income groups than do their nearest regular public schools. If we hold racial composition and low-income status constant—in effect, comparing charter schools and regular public schools with identical racial composition and income levels—the charter school advantage in the U.S. overall and in most states disappears, becoming substantially smaller, sometimes negative, and statistically insignificant.

On the other hand, the charter advantage remains important and significant in some states even after controlling for race and poverty. In Georgia, charter schools seem to maintain a statistically significant 5-point advantage; in Wisconsin they do even better. In New Jersey and Massachusetts, too, charter schools appear to have an edge, though the differences are not statistically significant.

There is now no longer any meaningful charter school advantage in either the central cities or their urban fringes.

Overall, one can conclude that controlling for race and poverty significantly reduces charter schools' proficiency advantage, both at the national level and for individual states. Of the major charter states, only California manages to have a significant charter school advantage after controlling for student characteristics.

Math Results

Hoxby's estimates imply that, for the nation as a whole, about 3 percentage points more students in charter schools are proficient in math, compared to their matched regular public schools. However, the 3-point advantage drops sharply when race and income are taken into account. . . .

The charter school advantage for math is lower than that for reading at the national level and tends to be lower at the state level as well. Of the nine major charter states (California, Michigan, Florida, Arizona, Texas, North Carolina, Colorado, Ohio, and Pennsylvania), none has a charter school proficiency advantage that is statistically significant once race and poverty are controlled for. In fact, only two out of the nine—Colorado and California—show a positive (though insignificant) charter coefficient when controlling just for race. . . .

Urban Charter Students and Achievement

It is often argued that charter schools serve a disproportionate number of central and inner-city children and that they are particularly effective in helping these overwhelmingly poor and minority students. Indeed. CCD [Common Core of Data] survey data confirm that charter schools are more likely to serve urban populations. Most are located either in large cities (35%) and their urban fringes (25%), or in mid-size cities (17%) and their urban fringes (8%). . . .

When one directly takes into account racial composition and poverty (proxied by free and reduced-price lunch eligibility) the perceived advantage of charter schools vanishes.

With no other controls, charter schools seem to enjoy an advantage over public schools in reading regardless of location. The effect in the urban fringe is the largest, exceeding the (aggregate) effect for the nation as a whole. The advantage for central cities becomes much smaller when Washington, D.C., is taken out, but it is still significant. But the addition of controls for race and income reduces the charter school advantage in all locales to the point where the effect is no longer statistically significant. In particular, there is now no longer any meaningful charter school advantage in either the central cities or their urban fringes.

The results for mathematics are similar. Under Hoxby's methodology, i.e., with no other controls, there is a small charter school advantage in the urban fringes (and a marginally significant effect for central cities, though this appears to be due mostly to Washington D.C.). But there is no charter school advantage in math in any locale once the analysis introduces a direct control for student racial composition and/or poverty.

The results for the distance sample . . . are similar. Initially, charter schools seem to hold a significant advantage over regular public schools in central cities and urban fringes for reading and in urban fringes for mathematics. Once race and poverty are taken into account, the advantage disappears—for mathematics the charter school effect is mostly negative, though the difference is statistically insignificant. . . .

In "A Straightforward Comparison of Charter Schools and Regular Public Schools in the United States," Caroline Hoxby argued that charter school students were 3.8% more likely to be proficient on their state's reading exam when compared to students in the nearest public school. They were 4.9% more likely to be proficient when compared to students in the nearest public school with a similar racial composition. The corresponding "charter advantage" in math was 1.6% and 2.8%. But Hoxby's method of matching schools based primarily on distance inadequately controls for differences in racial composition and socioeconomic status. When one directly takes into account racial composition and poverty (proxied by free and reduced-price lunch eligibility), the perceived advantage of charter schools vanishes. In math, in fact, the coefficient becomes negative in some cases, though it is not statistically significant. This is true not only for the U.S. as a whole and most of the major charter states, but also for charter schools in different locales, e.g., central cities and rural areas.

In retrospect, this is perhaps not surprising. When Hoxby matches charter schools with their nearest public schools *with a similar racial composition* instead of matching them with just the nearest public schools, the charter school advantage appears much larger. For example, in reading the estimate increases from 3.8% to 4.9% (an increase of about 30%), and in mathematics the increase is from 1.6% to 2.8% (an increase of about 75%). This is despite the fact that only about 8% of the schools differ between the two samples. That such a large change occurs by switching such a small number of schools in the sample underscores the importance of adequately controlling for racial composition and similar background variables—the results are likely to be seriously biased otherwise.

A cross-sectional study such as this one has its limitations, particularly in assigning causality based on the estimates. As is now widely accepted, the ideal way to determine effectiveness of policy changes or reform proposals is to randomize across students, and then follow the treatment and control groups over time. However, it is difficult to randomize on a large scale, and results can be sensitive to students leaving the study population as it progresses from year to year. It is often difficult even to gather longitudinal data on students by following the same students over time, and the problem of selection may not be satisfactorily resolved by a simple tracking of students over time. In the absence of adequate randomized trials and panel data, careful cross-sectional studies can often throw up interesting insights and alert us to potential problems and solutions, particularly when the sample is large and diverse enough. But their ability to expand our particular knowledge of what works and what doesn't in education is severely limited.

Charter Schools Help Close the Achievement Gap

The Education Innovator

The Education Innovator is a publication of the United States Department of Education.

Although progress has been made in elementary schools at narrowing the gap between low income, minority students and their white counterparts, secondary education has not followed suit. Several charter schools, including North Star Academy Charter School of Newark, demonstrate promise in closing the achievement gap in high schools. At North Star, for example, 99 percent of the students are African American or Hispanic. Graduating seniors from North Star have the highest rate of college acceptance of any school in New Jersey, demonstrating that the school has been able to close the achievement gap for its students. North Star and other selected charter high schools can serve as a model for the nation.

Albert Einstein once said, "You do not get out of a problem by using the same consciousness that got you into it." This statement is, perhaps, as true for problems of logic and science as it is for problems of education reform. For decades, the United States has grappled with pernicious achievement gaps that separate the academic performance of low-income, special needs, and minority students from their peers. Although progress has been made at the elementary level, there

The Education Innovator, "A New Guide Details How Charter High Schools Are Closing the Achievement Gap," vol. 4, November 7, 2006. Copyright 2006 ED.gov. Reproduced by permission.

is still work to do to improve the performance of students at the secondary level. To bring promising practices at the secondary level to light, the latest *Innovations in Education* guide from the U.S. Department of Education's Office of Innovation and Improvement focuses on eight charter high schools. These charter schools are bringing a new consciousness to the problem of raising the achievement of traditionally underserved student populations. The schools use innovative instructional practices, and many have completely re-tooled the traditional academic day and year to demonstrate that all students, regardless of their zip code, learning differences, race, or native language can become learners who are prepared to succeed in school and in life.

Charter schools, in particular, may be well suited to contribute to this cause. Charter schools are public schools, but they operate with more freedom than their traditional public school counterparts. Although levels of charter school autonomy vary from state to state, these schools generally are exempt from many state regulations in exchange for strict accountability for results. For example, charter schools often exercise greater control over their budgets, they may have more input regarding staffing decisions, and they have the ability to initiate cutting-edge programs.

Model Charter High Schools

As a result of charter schools' potential to improve the educational establishment as well as the prospects of students who need innovative, effective instructional programs the most, the latest *Innovations in Education* guide focuses on charter high schools closing the achievement gap. The schools included in the guide were chosen in 2005 from over 400 charter high schools that are meeting academic targets under the No Child Left Behind Act (NCLB) and are closing achievement gaps by holding students to high academic standards. To be considered, the schools had to have graduated at least one cohort of students and have data to show that, for the most part, students were moving on to postsecondary education or employment. Eight schools were ultimately selected for the guide: Gateway High School (CA), Media and Technology Charter High School (MA), Minnesota New Country School (MN), The Preuss School (CA), The SEED Public Charter School (DC), Toledo School for the Arts (OH), YES College Preparatory School (TX), and North Star Academy Charter School of Newark (NJ). Each of these schools is college preparatory in intent, and each is developing creative solutions to problems faced by high schools across the country.

Along with a relentless focus on goals, these schools also work to build a positive school culture where students and staff feel valued.

Although all the schools are unique, six similar characteristics unite them. Across the board, the schools are mission-driven; focus on college preparation; teach for mastery; provide support; value professional learning; and hold themselves accountable.

The first unifying factor among the schools is that they are mission-driven because they were created in response to what their founders believed was a lack of high-quality secondary school options in their local communities. Because the schools were created with the intent of meeting students' needs as their primary objective, teachers, school leaders, parents, board members, and community partners maintain a laser-like focus on ensuring that their missions ensure students' success. All adults have a clear understanding of and commitment to the mission of their schools, and all decisions from staffing to budget allocations are made based on whether the mission is furthered. Along with a relentless focus on goals, these schools also work to build a positive school culture where students and staff feel valued.

Rigorous Curricula

One way of ensuring that students feel valued is to offer them a rigorous, college-preparatory curriculum that keeps them engaged and excited about learning. Most of the profiled schools offer Advanced Placement courses along with additional support services. In these schools, there is no such thing as a "college track;" there is only a "success track." In addition to academic rigor, the schools promote internships and enrichment opportunities that allow students to apply the lessons they learn in the classroom to experiences that enhance their understanding of the world that extends beyond their local communities.

To ensure that all their students are prepared for higher education and the "real world," teachers in the profiled schools teach for mastery, expect their students to work hard, and do not accept social promotion. If learning requires more time than a teacher initially anticipated, more time is provided. Lesson plans are flexible, evolving instructional guides—not documents set in the stone of an immovable curricular timeline. All schools have developed longer academic days or years, and some have added summer and weekend sessions.

The high graduation and college-going rates at these profiled schools belie the notion that traditionally underserved students cannot perform to high standards.

Support for Students and Teachers

It is important to note that these schools not only offer students more rigor and more time on task—they also offer more support. This support is exemplified in advisory programs, academic tutoring, mentoring, and college counseling. Each of the schools provides a relatively low student-to-teacher ratio (22:1) and employs part-time specialists, social workers, special education teachers, and parent volunteers who work daily with students. Indeed, parents are considered an invaluable resource at these schools, whether they are serving on the governing boards, fundraising, or participating in parent-teacher conferences.

The idea of support also extends to teachers. A number of the schools have built in regular opportunities either during the academic day or year for teachers to plan, reflect, and collaborate with one another. The principals at these schools value professional learning by working closely with teachers to improve instruction. Principals act as instructional leaders by conducting classroom observations, providing feedback on lesson plans, and collaboratively organizing intervention strategies for struggling students.

School Accountability

The final unifying factor among these schools is that they hold themselves accountable. Strong, active governing boards are at the helm of these schools, generating creative solutions to problems and empowering school leaders to make and implement decisions in a manner that is both expeditious and beneficial to students. The schools are fiscally responsible, and they regularly use student achievement data and information gathered from their constituents to improve their operations.

The high graduation and college-going rates at these profiled schools belie the notion that traditionally underserved students cannot perform to high standards. One of the profiled schools, North Star Academy Charter School of Newark (NJ), named for Frederick Douglass' abolitionist paper *The North Star*, promotes higher education as the guiding "North Star" of success for its inner-city students, the majority of whom are African-American. The story of North Star Academy begins with James Verrilli, a teacher in the Newark public schools, and Norman Atkins, a journalist with a private foundation, both of whom set out to improve the gloomy outlook for students living in the second poorest city in the United

States. In 1997, the year that North Star was founded, only 50 percent of freshmen that enrolled in Newark high schools reached their senior year and, of those, only 26 percent planned to attend college, six percent actually enrolled, and only two percent earned degrees. Now in its ninth year of operation, North Star is improving the life chances of Newark students with its 100 percent graduation rate and 95 percent college-going rate for the class of 2005.

With the highest rate of four-year college acceptance and attendance of any school in New Jersey, North Star has truly become a guiding light for Newark's most needy students.

A Profile of North Star Academy

North Star began as a middle school, but was expanded to serve high school students at the request of local parents who wanted better school options for their students after the eighth grade. The school currently [as of 2006] serves 384 students in fifth through twelfth grade, with 125 students in the high school section. Ninety-nine percent of the students are African-American or Hispanic. All students who are accepted through the school's lottery system understand that they will be required to work hard throughout North Star's 11-month academic year. To graduate, students must take four years of English, mathematics, science, and history, and three years of foreign language, physical education, and the arts. North Star also encourages its students to enroll in Advanced Placement calculus, U.S. history, U.S. government, and English. None of the classes at North Star are tracked in terms of academic rigor because all classes offer honors-level, college-preparatory work. Additional graduation requirements include passing the New Jersey High School Proficiency Assessment, completing a senior thesis and composition, taking the SAT at least twice, engaging in 40 hours of community service, and applying to at least two colleges.

As if North Star students were not busy enough, the school also offers internships and special programs. For example, there is a journalism project in partnership with Princeton University, a Junior Statesman program through Georgetown University, and an FBI [Federal Bureau of Investigation] Summer Training Institute. Students who keep up their grades may spend a month off campus on work sites or traveling to foreign countries. Through a partnership with AFS Intercultural Programs, Inc., North Star students can spend time in China, Paraguay, Costa Rica, and Argentina. A relationship with VISIONS Service Adventures enables students to volunteer in Ecuador and the Dominican Republic.

North Star's Innovation

Two of North Star's most innovative features are its use of data to inform instruction and its commitment to ensuring that all students understand the subject matter they are taught. Every six to eight weeks, teachers administer a set of interim assessments that are aligned with state standards and the school's curriculum. Teachers, department chairs, and the school principal examine the results and determine which students need additional help. Teachers then re-teach key concepts to the whole class or offer tutoring to individual students before, during, or after the school day. North Star also offers a Saturday tutoring session, so that no student slips behind. Another distinctive element at the school is the principal's presence as an instructional leader. Every day, high school principal Julie Jackson and the principal at North Star's sister middle school visit at least 85 percent of classrooms. The principals observe classes, provide informal feedback to teachers, and use data from the interim assessments to draw connections between instruction and student learning.

The hard work of principals, teachers, and students at North Star Academy Charter School of Newark appears to be paying off, with 100 percent of twelfth grade students in the class of 2005 passing the New Jersey High School Statewide Assessment, compared to 85.1 percent of students statewide, 44.2 percent of students in the district, and 19.5 percent of students in neighborhood schools. With the highest rate of four-year college acceptance and attendance of any school in New Jersey, North Star has truly become a guiding light for Newark's most needy students and a model for other schools across the country trying to eliminate the achievement gap.

13

Charter Schools Do Not Address the Achievement Gap

Ron Zimmer and Richard Buddin

Ron Zimmer is a policy analyst and Richard Buddin is a senior economist. Both work for the Rand Corporation.

Educational reformers believe that charter schools may be able to close the gap in achievement between students of different races and socioeconomic levels. Measuring schools' success in closing the gap, however, has been notoriously difficult. Using student-level data, followed over a long period of time, researchers examined two urban school districts in California. Their analysis reveals that charter schools increase segregation. In addition, the effect of being in a charter school appears to do little to increase achievement in individual students. Indeed, it appears that charter schools are not improving student learning at a greater rate than traditional public schools and are therefore not closing the achievement gap.

In the national drive to improve school learning, urban school districts pose some of the greatest challenges. These districts serve the vast majority of poor, minority, and immigrant children in the country. As various achievement indicators have begun to creep upward for the nation as a whole, poor and minority students have largely been bypassed, and early gains in reducing achievement gaps have not been maintained. Achievement levels are low in urban districts, even when controlling for their level of poverty.

Ron Zimmer and Richard Buddin, *Charter School Performance in Urban Districts,* Danvers, MA: Rand Education Working Papers, 2005. http://www.rand.org/pubs/ working_papers/2005/RAND_WR282.pdf. Republished with permission of Rand Corporation, conveyed through Copyright Clearance Center, Inc.

Do Charter Schools Help Urban Students?

While a number of curriculum, professional development, and leadership reforms have been instituted to address the challenges in urban districts across the country, some reformers, including mayors of some of the largest cities, are looking to charter schools as a mechanism of fundamental change for improving student achievement. Charter schools, which are publicly supported, autonomously operated schools of choice, now educate a significant portion of many of the major urban school districts' students including Cincinnati, Columbus, Dayton, Detroit, Los Angeles, Kansas City, Milwaukee, Phoenix, San Diego, and Washington. In addition, initiatives are in place to expand the role of charter schools in other major urban districts including Chicago, New York, and Indianapolis.

Recent analyses have examined the statewide performance of charter schools in Arizona, California, Michigan, North Carolina, and Texas. However, there is little research on the performance of charter schools in urban environments or on the effects of charter schools on students disaggregated by various demographic characteristics, including race/ethnicity.

In this [viewpoint], we examine the performance of charter schools in the nation's 2nd and 15th largest school districts, Los Angeles Unified School District and San Diego Unified School Districts—both for all students in these charter schools and for students grouped by limited English proficiency status and race/ethnicity. Currently [as of 2005], Los Angeles has 49 charter schools, enrolling over 25,000 students, while San Diego has 21 charter schools enrolling over 9,000 students. These charter schools often serve a disproportionate share of minority students and advocates hope to reduce the prevailing achievement gap between minority and nonminority students. This paper uses student-level data to examine the progress charter schools are making in achieving this objective.

The Charter School Movement

Since its inception in 1991, the charter school movement has seen tremendous growth as 40 states and the District of Columbia have passed charter school laws. There are now over 3,400 charter schools enrolling nearly 1 million students nationwide. As the charter school movement has grown, rhetoric from advocates and opponents has dominated the debate. Supporters hope that charter schools will be able to cut through red tape and offer innovative and effective educational programs, provide new options to families (especially low-income and minority families), and promote healthy competition for traditional public schools. Opponents argue that charter schools are no more effective than traditional public schools, that they may exacerbate racial segregation, that they create fiscal strains for school districts, and that too many of them are fly-by-night operations.

Charter schools lead to greater segregation by race and . . . charter schools have a negative effect on the performance of both black and white students.

Only recently have researchers been able to provide any quantifiable results. While some of this research has relied upon school-level data or point-in-time data of a cross section of charter and traditional public schools, the most reliable results have used student-level data. A key weakness of a school-level analysis is the high degree of aggregation [grouping together], which masks changes over time in the school's population of students and variation of performance across different subjects and grades. In essence, school-level data may not pick up the nuances of school characteristics and can only provide an incomplete picture of why outcomes vary across schools. Similarly, point-in-time data, even if it is student-level, do not account for the amount of time spent in different schools and factor out the various non-school forces at work. Dealing with this methodological problem is challenging under any circumstances, and it is especially problematic in evaluating charter schools, where students are likely to differ from those in traditional public schools simply because they have chosen to attend charter schools. These differences between choosing and non-choosing students may be related to achievement in positive or negative ways, thereby producing "selection bias" in comparing achievement in charter schools and traditional public schools.

One way of dealing with selection bias is to collect longitudinal student-level data [following individual students over time]. Longitudinal designs minimize the problem of selection bias by examining the academic gains made by individual students over time, factoring out students' baseline achievement levels. Moreover, they permit "within-student" comparisons of achievement gains, examining changes in the achievement trajectories of individual students who move from traditional public schools to charter schools, or vice versa.

Longitudinal, panel data sets for individual students have been used in state-level studies of charter schools.... These studies, however, have not yet converged to produce a clear and consistent finding about the academic effectiveness of charter schools. Furthermore, these studies have focused on statewide charter performance and have not focused on urban environments or the performance of charter students by demographic characteristics.

One notable exception to these statewide analyses is [Caroline M.] Hoxby and [Jonah] Rockoff's examination of three charter schools in Chicago, which provided some evidence that charter students outperform non-charter students. Their analysis capitalized on the fact that these schools are oversubscribed and used a lottery mechanism to admit students. Presumably the lottery winners and losers are similar in every way except admission into these schools. Tracking performance of both sets of students then creates an unbiased perspective of performance. However, Hoxby and Rockoff's study has one major drawback. While it provides the best possible evaluation for those schools included in the evaluation, it may have limited implications for those schools that do not have wait lists. In fact, you would expect schools with wait lists to be the best schools, and it would be surprising if they had the same results as charter schools without wait lists.

Our results suggest that charter schools are not consistently producing improved test scores for minorities above and beyond traditional public schools.

Also worthy of note is a more recent paper by [Robert] Bifulco and [Helen F.] Ladd in which they examine the effect charter schools in North Carolina have on the distribution and achievement of students by race. Again, using a longitudinal student-level data set, the authors find that charter schools lead to greater segregation by race and that charter schools have a negative effect on the performance of both black and white students, but the effect for blacks is substantially larger than the effect for whites. They attribute these large negative effects for blacks to the segregation of blacks into charter schools.

In our analysis . . . we examine the performance of charter schools for students of different demographic characteristics, using longitudinally linked student level data in two major urban districts of Los Angeles and San Diego. Given the chronic challenge of reducing achievement gaps for disadvantaged students in urban environments, our results have strong implications for policymakers and educators.

Our results show that charter schools are doing little to improve the test scores of their students in Los Angeles and San Diego. The elementary school results show that Los Angeles charter students are keeping pace with traditional school students in reading and math, but charter students are lagging behind their traditional school counterparts in San Diego. At the secondary-school level, Los Angeles charter students score slightly higher than traditional school students in reading and slightly lower in math. The test score pattern across reading and math is reversed in San Diego. In all cases, the charter school effect is small compared to the overall annual trend in test scores.

The results show only small differences in charter effects across race/ethnic and LEP [limited English proficiency] groups of students. One of the strongest rationales for charter schools, and school choice generally, is that choice gives greater opportunities for disadvantaged students, primarily minority students. In some cases, political and district leaders have bought into the charter philosophy in hopes of closing the achievement gap of minority and non-minority students. One result suggests that charter schools are not consistently producing improved test scores for minorities above and beyond traditional public schools. Charter schools may have positive effects on other outcomes that are not assessed here, such as safety and curriculum breadth, but charter schools in Los Angeles and San Diego are not showing pervasive gains in student test scores.

14

Charter Schools Hold Hope for the Future

Chester E. Finn Jr. and Gregg Vanourek

Chester E. Finn Jr. is the president of the Thomas B. Fordham Institute, an educational research foundation. Gregg Vanourek was formerly associated with the Thomas B. Fordham Institute and is now the chief executive officer of Vanourek Consulting Solutions, LLC, an educational consulting firm.

Charter schools demonstrate how the private sector can work with and for public education. This private/public partnership offers hope for the educational future of the United States. Charter schools offer strict accountability in exchange for freedom from rules and regulations. Because of this trade-off, they are able to experiment and innovate in ways that traditional schools cannot. The competition provided by charter schools also improves the quality of education at traditional schools, which must attract students to remain viable. Imagination, innovation, and accountability will work together to provide the kind of education the United States needs in the twenty-first century.

Public charter schools offer today's most dramatic example of mobilizing the private sector on behalf of public education in the United States. The charter movement is a dynamic example of how an essential government function that has been recycled with few fundamental changes for well over a century can be reconceived to accommodate entrepreneurial

Chester E. Finn Jr. and Gregg Vanourek, *Lessons from the U.S. Experience with Charter Schools—PEPG 05-10* Cambridge, MA: PEPG, Harvard University, Kennedy School of Government, 2006. Reproduced by permission.

initiative, private-sector investment, competitive forces, the profit motive, performance contracting, franchising, and more—all within the context of public funding, standards, and oversight. More than that, the practice of "chartering schools" provides a compelling example of how the entire U.S. education enterprise can be redesigned. In this essay, we review the background of charter schooling, examine how charter schools are doing in 2005, and draw a series of lessons about the nexus of public and private forces in chartering.

Charter Schools: Freedom and Accountability

Charter schools are independent public schools of choice, freed from many regulations yet accountable for their results. A group of parents, educators, or entrepreneurs (or combinations thereof) can develop the vision for a school (wholly new or the conversion of an existing school) and apply (through a formal, prescribed process) to a charter authorizer (a gatekeeper or licensing body) to run a school that will be open to all children in a defined area (sometimes a school district, sometimes an entire state). If awarded a charter—a performance contract authorizing the school to operate for a set period of time (usually five years)—this founding coalition forms a board of trustees that then hires staff to launch and operate the school. Every such school must follow the requirements of its state's charter law, including compliance with nondiscrimination norms, mandatory testing, pupil attendance, and the like. After the initial charter term is up, the school must return to its authorizer and seek renewal of its charter based on its demonstrated performance—or face sanctions or even closure.

At the heart of the charter model is a bargain: eased restrictions meant to free educators from red tape and inefficiencies in exchange for tightened accountability for academic performance at the school level. This "tight-loose" framework entails a drastic shift, even a reversal, in American educational governance, which has long concerned itself with the micro-regulation of school inputs and processes while neglecting results. And this new framework has special salience at a time when the United States is seeking to "leave no child behind" and when the most important thing to know about a school is what results it is producing. . . .

Charter schools can be thought of as a "license to dream" for educators and entrepreneurs seeking to improve on the current state of the art.

Charter schooling can be seen as a form of "reinventing government," a popular concept in the U.S. in the 1990s whereby government entities embraced private-sector dynamics to improve their efficiency and performance. Essentially, public agencies were being asked to "steer, not row"—that is, to set policy goals and frameworks but rely on other organizations, often specialized private or nonprofit groups, to run programs and deliver services. The idea was that competitive outsourcing would drive efficiencies and give customers (in this case, families) what they seek. . . .

Chartering Will Improve Education

Chartering incorporates a theory of organizational change in public education, too: that creating sound school choices will improve educational quality in two ways: 1) by supplying immediate alternatives to students who are not thriving in their present schools, and 2) by exerting competitive pressure on the system to improve while providing it with innovative examples of schools that work.

Twenty years ago, the United States lacked imagination about public schools. They were assumed to be near-permanent institutions of brick and mortar. Like libraries, parks, or churches, they were expected to last practically forever, and it was not uncommon for children to attend their parents' school. Regrettably, many of those immortal institutions were not getting the job done and failing to keep pace with technological innovations, organizational breakthroughs, and fast-changing delivery systems. Yet for a host of reasons it was extremely difficult to change them—and then only on the margin. Perhaps creating new ones was a more promising approach.

Chartering went beyond this "new school strategy" by introducing the important innovation of the "authorizer" in lieu of the "central office"—that is, entities are empowered to "sponsor" charter schools and hold them to account under terms of their charters, which are essentially performance contracts. In time, many such entities came to fill this authorizing role, including not only local school districts but also colleges and universities, state agencies, a mayor's office, and specialized nonprofit organizations (all depending on the state charter law).

Charter schools . . . have importance not only for particular communities and families but also for the evolution of public education itself, whose DNA is gradually being altered.

Charter Schools Are Changing Ideas

At the micro level, charter schools can be thought of as a "license to dream" for educators and entrepreneurs seeking to improve on the current state of the art—and an outlet for struggling schoolchildren stuck in stultifying neighborhood schools. At the macro level, charter schools are transforming our definition of "public" schools by demonstrating that they need not be administered in top-down fashion by bureaucratic bodies. Rather, a school is public so long as it is open to all members of the public in nondiscriminatory fashion, paid for by the public via tax dollars, and accountable to public agencies for its academic performance and stewardship of funds. Yet this concept is so new that most charter school debates are still framed erroneously as a struggle between "charter" and "public" schools, even though charter schools are, by definition, *public* schools.

The Components of Chartering

Charter schools, then, have importance not only for particular communities and families but also for the evolution of public education itself, whose DNA is gradually being altered by the ten essential components of the charter model:

1. *Site-based governance*: Chartering begins with community-based, "locus-of-control" governance of public schools, with charter school boards independent of existing bureaucracies but still accountable to government officials and the electorate.

2. *Deregulation*: Charter schools are offered freedom from red tape that ensnarls traditional public schooling, allowing their leaders and teachers to shift their focus from compliance to learning.

3. *Entrepreneurial talent*: The chartering opportunity attracts talent from beyond the traditional education sector (and unearths it from within), infusing fresh thinking about how to design, operate, and sustain high-performing schools.

4. *Experimentation*: As they offer alternatives, charters try new approaches to schooling—from curriculum and instruction to culture, leadership, governance, technology, parental involvement, contracting, partnerships, and structure, as well as the length and flow of the school day and year. Charters have agility and originality that district-run schools, at least in a particular locale, often lack. In the charter world, for example, we are far more apt to find teacher-run schools, employer-run schools, and cyber schools.

5. *Choice*: The presence of charter schools in a community allows parents to select schools that meet their children's needs as well as their own priorities—and allows educators to opt for new arrangements that suit them, too. Chartering implicitly rejects the "comprehensive school" model in which every school purports to be all things for all kids—inviting specialization within schools and diversity across schools.

6. *Competition*: When different school models are offered, each school must react to what other schools are doing, pay attention to what parents seek, and meet the academic and operating standards of the community. Otherwise, it faces obsolescence or marketplace extinction.

7. *Evaluation*: An essential component of chartering is assessing what works (and does not work) in education, so that educators, authorizers, and policymakers can make informed decisions. This requires regular assessments, transparent information, and agreed-upon performance norms.

8. *Accountability*: Holding schools to account for their academic results—as well as their legal compliance, operating efficiency, and financial viability—helps to ensure that failing schools are restructured or closed (the equivalent of filing for educational bankruptcy).

9. *Deployment*: As chartering yields successful models, these can be replicated so that excellence pervades the system while mediocrity is squeezed out. This dynamic restructuring process is imbued in the DNA of chartering—the prospect of educational excellence going viral.

10. *Renewal*: Through the deployment process, contingent upon successful execution of the prior components of chartering, we can expect a renewed system of schools that self-corrects over time, "learning" how to get better. . . .

How Are Charters Doing?

The most complete and recent picture [of charter school achievement] is presented in a meta-analysis of 44 major studies, released in July 2005 by Dr. Bryan Hassel and the National Alliance for Public Charter Schools, which draws conclusions in three areas.

Chartering holds promise as an approach to getting better schools. What we have is an experiment worth continuing—and refining.

First, diversity of outcomes. Results vary widely from one school to another, with some charters at the top in their communities, others at the bottom, and many in the middle. This range complicates all discussions of charter schools' performance. Some of America's highest-performing schools are charters, with examples visible in such places as Boston, San Diego, Chicago, New York City, and Washington, D.C. At the same time, plenty of charter schools reveal dismal academic results.

Second, evidence of "added value." Of the 26 studies that sought to appraise change in student performance over time, Hassel reports, 12 found charters with larger overall gains than district schools, four found larger gains in certain categories, and six found comparable gains. (Four other studies found lesser gains in charters.)

Third, most studies indicate that charter schools' performance improves over time. Five of seven studies find that more mature schools do better. Hassel's conclusion: "Chartering holds promise as an approach to getting better schools. What we have is an experiment worth continuing—and refining."

Other Accomplishments

Beyond academic performance, we can point to seven significant accomplishments of the U.S. charter venture so far:

1. *Providing new opportunities for struggling students.* Charter schools enroll a large proportion of underserved students, especially poor and minority youngsters for whom there exists a stubborn achievement gap. At a time when the U.S. is striving to "leave no child behind" and when that goal includes creating alternatives for children trapped in failing schools, chartering is an especially good way to supply new options, especially in urban areas.

2. *Creating high levels of parent involvement and community support.* Many charter schools make extensive use of parent volunteers, with parents serving on school governing boards and with some schools asking parents to sign contracts affirming their commitment to their children's academic success. Reports the U.S. Department of Education, "Charter schools are more likely than traditional public schools to have high levels of parental involvement in the areas of budget decisions, governance, instructional issues, parent education workshops, and volunteering."

3. *Fostering educational innovation.* Besides a new governance model, many charter schools bring curricular diversification to their communities; some experiment with organizational structure (e.g., school or class size, "schools within schools," residential campuses for troubled children), and some charter schools are celebrated for their demanding but supportive school culture (e.g., the acclaimed Knowledge Is Power Program, or KIPP). The charter sector also seems to be an "early adopter" of new technologies and instructional delivery methods such as "virtual" schools that operate primarily in cyberspace.

4. *Encouraging entrepreneurialism.* Chartering attracts entrepreneurs and committed reformers who wouldn't otherwise be in public education. New York City school chancellor Joel Klein likes charter schools because they "bring in new blood. These are leaders and entrepreneurs who are not otherwise part of the system. They are people with ideas, with creativity, and who are willing to give their all for their students." A new "charter industry" is beginning to emerge, bustling with activity among for-profit and non-profit service providers, networks, contractors, and more.

5. *Leveraging private capital.* Both through private investment and philanthropy, chartering attracts many millions of dollars to augment government funds—from for-profit and non-profit management organizations to associations, resource centers, charitable foundations, donors, venture funds, lenders, and more.

6. *Boosting efficiency.* Charters receive far fewer dollars than district-operated public schools. According to an August 2005 study, "On average, . . . charter funding fell short of district funding by $1,801 per pupil, or 21.7 percent" in the 17 states studied, with funding disparities ranging from 39.5 percent (South Carolina) to 4.8 percent (New Mexico). Having to make bricks with less straw is onerous and sometimes counter-productive, but it can also yield cost savings, and productivity gains—especially where charter school performance rivals or surpasses district schools, essentially offering "more bang for the buck."

7. *Deploying market forces.* Chartering avails itself of competitive pressure to shape and drive the education enterprise, ration resources, and instill accountability for performance. To remain viable, a charter school must attract and retain families. Parents can "vote with their

feet" by shunning or exiting their local charter school. The robust deployment of market forces is significant in a sector where almost nothing operates at scale, incentives for compliance trump those for performance, organizations are politicized instead of optimized, and R&D [research and development] is not even a line item in the typical district budget. . . .

With chartering we're beginning to witness a profound shift in basic assumptions about what a public school is and the ground rules by which it operates (or expires).

The Future of Chartering

What does the future hold for U.S. charter schools—and for public schooling in the era of chartering? Large governmental bureaucracies may continue to define education standards and measure school results, but they will have less control over the *delivery* of K-12 education services, as has long been true of American tertiary education and countless other sectors of our mixed-market economy.

And why not? In a time when communist China, run by an old guard of command-and-control devotees in Beijing, is plunging into market-oriented economics and private-sector investment, initiative, and technology, the prospect of the American education behemoth mobilizing the private sector via "third way" solutions is not far-fetched.

At minimum, today's new schools are a needed tonic for the old ones. It also seems likely, however, that with chartering we're beginning to witness a profound shift in basic assumptions about what a public school is and the ground rules by which it operates (or expires). The institutional and accountability innovations that chartering brings may be laying the foundation for a redesigned structure of public education as a whole. In that new architecture, successful schools are incubated and brought to scale, entrepreneurs introduce fresh ideas (and resources) into the sector, overseers of schools (perhaps altogether new entities) steer them in wise policy directions but leave others to row, authorizers hold schools strictly to account for their results (not their intentions, inputs, or processes), parents carefully choose among many varieties of educational enterprises, and schools boost their performance via dynamic leadership, effective instruction and governance, organizational efficiency, and smart use of new technologies and delivery systems. The result—and what makes all the sturm und drang [turmoil] worth it—will be a better educated populace that meets the nation's 21st century needs and helps all its residents achieve the successful and rewarding lives that are their birthright.

15

The Charter Movement
Is a Broken Promise

New York State United Teachers

The New York State United Teachers is a teachers' union affiliated with the American Federation of Teachers, the National Education Association, and the AFL-CIO.

The New York State Legislature created charter schools in 1998. At that time, a cap was placed on the number of charter schools that could be opened. At the end of 2006, that number was reached, and the legislature began consideration of whether to raise the cap. The cap should not be raised, however, because there is not clear evidence that charter schools are better than traditional public schools. In addition, charter schools do not offer what they promised in the way of expanded learning opportunities, nor do they provide greater student achievement. Instead, they damage local public schools. Charter schools are failing students and taxpayers and should be limited in number.

In December of 1998, the [New York State] Legislature adopted and [New York] Gov. George Pataki signed into law the New York Charter Schools Act of 1998, which said the purpose of the new schools would be to:

- Improve student learning and achievement;

- Increase learning opportunities for all students, with special emphasis on expanded learning experiences for students who are at risk of academic failure;

- Encourage the use of different and innovative teaching methods;

- Create new professional opportunities for teachers, school administrators, and other school personnel;

- Provide parents and students with expanded choices in the types of educational opportunities that are available within the public school system; and

- Provide schools with a method of change from rules-based to performance-based accountability systems by holding schools established under this article accountable for meeting measurable student achievement results.

The law allowed the State Board of Regents and the SUNY [State University of New York] Board of Trustees to set up a total of 100 charter schools in New York State, a cap that was reached during the 2005–06 school year. This year [2006] the Governor is proposing to raise the cap to 250 charter schools. Before legislators consider any expansion of the charter school experiment, it is imperative to review how these schools are performing—in light of the criteria the Legislature established, and in comparison to comparable public schools in their districts. As this report demonstrates, the charter school experiment is falling far short of the promise the Legislature intended.

Charter Schools Are Falling Short

The most powerful evidence available—student scores on state tests—clearly demonstrates that charter schools are falling short of the purposes the Legislature intended. The failed promise of the charter school experiment too often has been overlooked because of widespread misperceptions—fueled by government-funded charter advertising campaigns—that charters perform better than their public school counterparts. This is not true. Charter school proponents use misleading statistics to suggest success. Charter schools typically enroll students who are more advantaged than the student population in their districts and they enroll fewer special education students or English language learners than public schools in their home districts. When each charter school's performance is compared with a comparable public school from their home district—when the schools are matched in terms of student poverty—*fully 86.4 percent of the comparable public schools equal or best the charter school* in a side-by-side comparison. Put another way, only 13.6 percent of charter schools are performing better than their public counterpart—results too disappointing to warrant expanding the experiment. It would be folly to increase the number of charter schools before thoroughly examining the reasons why they have fallen short of the promise they were created to fulfill.

Charter schools are not offering expanded learning opportunities to at-risk students and, in fact, tend to serve students who are more advantaged than the population of their district.

---

1. Contrary to the claims of charter school advocates, charter schools are *not* surpassing public schools in improving student learning and achievement. In a side-by-side comparison of each charter school with a comparable public school in the same district, fully 86.4 percent of the public schools equaled or surpassed the charter school's performance. Only six charter schools (13.6 percent) had student achievement on state tests that outperformed the comparable public school in their home school district.

2. Charter school advocates typically avoid comparing their student test scores with comparable public schools. Instead, they seek to compare their performance with their

district as a whole, an unfair comparison because district test results include significantly more special ed students, significantly more financially disadvantaged students and significantly more students who are English language learners than the charter schools in their midst.

3. Charter schools are not offering expanded learning opportunities to at-risk students and, in fact, tend to serve students who are more advantaged than the population of their district. A key measure of poverty is the percentage of students receiving publicly subsidized free or reduced price lunch. Only 17 charter schools serve a higher percentage of students on free lunch than the home school district and only two charter schools serve a higher percentage of students on free lunch than any school in the home school district. Charter schools, in fact, tend to serve students who are less needy than the general student population in their home districts.

4. Based on the State Education Department *Annual Report on Charter Schools*, these schools are using educational approaches that are readily available to public schools, undercutting the state goal of innovation and enhanced options.

5. Charter schools are expected to offer professional opportunities to teachers, administrators and other school personnel that are not available in the public schools. In fact, there are anecdotal reports of significant staff turnover at most charter schools.

6. The test scores from charter schools indicate that charter schools do not offer parents and students better choices or results than are already available in public schools. Only 13.6 percent of the charter schools operating in 2004–05 have better test scores than comparable schools in their home school district.

7. Charter schools are not being held accountable to the same extent as public schools for student performance. Many charter schools have operated under the accountability radar by offering grades where state tests are not required. In 2004–05, 17 charter schools did not participate in the state testing system because they did not offer fourth or eighth grade. Only six charter schools did better on state tests than comparable public schools from their home school district. Public schools are performing better and are more accountable than charter schools.

This study of charter school performance shows charter schools have fallen short of the promise and purposes described in the legislation creating charter schools. The experiment is not working and should not be expanded by increasing the cap. Changes in the law should be made to take the financial burden off school districts where charters are located by enacting transition aid; and stronger accountability measures should be put in place to make charter schools more accountable to local communities and the state. Before any increase in the number of charter schools is even considered, a limit must be placed on the percentage of public school students enrolled in charter schools in an individual school district, as well as the percentage of public school budgets diverted to charter schools. This would help ameliorate the damaging effects of over-saturation of experimental charter schools in any one district.

Organizations to Contact

The editors have compiled the following list of organizations concerned with the issues debated in this book. The descriptions are derived from materials provided by the organizations. All have publications or information available for interested readers. The list was compiled on the date of publication of the present volume; the information provided here may change. Be aware that many organizations take several weeks or longer to respond to inquiries, so allow as much time as possible.

American Federation of Teachers, AFL-CIO
555 New Jersey Ave. NW, Washington, DC   20001
(202) 879-4400
Web site: www.aft.org

The American Federation of Teachers (AFT) is a labor union affiliated with the AFL-CIO and comprised of teachers at all levels. The AFT opposes charter schools and has sponsored significant research on the comparative achievement of charter school students and traditional public school students. These studies, as well as information on important legislative issues, are available at the AFT Web site.

Brookings Institution
1775 Massachusetts Ave. NW, Washington, DC   20036
(202) 797-6000 • fax: (202)797-6004
Web site: www.brookings.edu

The Brookings Institution is a think tank that tackles important national issues, including charter schools. The institution publishes books and policy briefs, all available on the Web site. Many publications regarding charter schools and school choice are available, along with links to other studies.

Center for American Progress
1333 H Street NW, 10th Floor, Washington, DC   20005

(202) 682-1611
e-mail: progress@americanprogress.org
Web site: www.americanprogress.org

The Center for American Progress is a "progressive think tank dedicated to improving the lives of Americans through ideas and action." The center works to affect public policy, including issues of education and charter schools. It publishes a variety of newsletters, available on the Web site, as well as research. The Web site has many resources for students studying charter schools.

Center for Education Reform

1001 Connecticut Ave. NW, Washington, DC   20036
(202) 822-9000 • fax: (202) 822-5077
Web site: www.edreform.com

The Center for Education Reform is an advocacy group and resource center for people interested in charter schools. The center publishes newsletters and operates a system whereby registrants can be notified by e-mail of breaking news and research studies. It maintains a searchable database of resources and charter schools. In addition, it posts "fast facts" on the Web page along with many links to other resources.

Center on Reinventing Public Education

Daniel J. Evans School of Public Affairs
University of Washington, Seattle, WA   98103-9158
(206) 685-2214 • fax: (206) 221-7402
e-mail: crpe@u.washington.edu
Web site: www.crpe.org

The Center on Reinventing Public Education is a resource center that conducts research and analysis on how to develop effective and accountable schools. The Center is the home of the National Charter School Research Project, which has assembled a database of charter school studies. The Web site has many downloadable articles and studies.

Education Commission of the States

700 Broadway, #1200, Denver, CO   80203-3450
(303) 299-3600 • fax: (303) 296-8332
e-mail: ecs@ecs.org
Web site: www.ecs.org

The motto of the Education Commission of the States is "helping state leaders shape education policy." It is a clearinghouse of information for policy makers, educators, researchers, and students. In addition to the Web site, it circulates two electronic publications: *e-Clips*, a daily roundup of the top education news, and *e-Connection*, a weekly bulletin. The commission also releases print resources every year; as of 2007, there were more than one hundred titles listed on the Web site.

Education/Evolving

451 East Kellogg Blvd., Saint Paul, MN   55101
(651) 789-3096 • fax: (651) 789 3098
e-mail: info@educationevolving.org
Web site: www.educationevolving.org

Education/Evolving is a Minnesota organization supporting new public charter schools started "from scratch" by parents, teachers, community organizations, and partnerships. The Web site provides useful information on educational change, particularly with regard to charter schools.

The Education Trust

1250 H Street NW, Suite 700, Washington, DC   20005
(202) 293-1217 • fax: (202) 293-2605
Web site: www2.edtrust.org

The Education Trust is an advocacy and resource center dedicated to "closing the achievement gaps that separate low-income students and students of color from other youth." The trust provides reports, resources, data, and policy information, all in full text on the Web site.

National Alliance for Public Charter Schools

1101 Fourteenth Street NW, Suite 801
Washington, DC   20005
(202) 289-2700 • fax: (202) 289-4009
Web site: www.publiccharters.org

The National Alliance for Public Charter Schools is an organization that advocates for the charter school movement. It is committed to increasing the number of charter schools and equalizing finances between charters and traditional public schools. It publishes *Issue Briefs* and other publications and holds a national conference each year. The Web site provides full text of news articles, research studies, and links to other helpful information.

National Education Association (NEA)

1201 Sixteenth Street NW, Washington, DC   20036-3290
(202) 833-4000 • fax: (202) 822-7974
Web site: www.nea.org

The National Education Association is an advocacy group and union comprised of educators at all levels. The NEA is generally opposed to charter schools being exempt from teacher certification regulations and has issued a policy statement on charter schools that is available on its Web site. In addition, the NEA publishes a free e-mail newsletter. The Web site contains articles on issues in education as well as reports on recent legislation affecting public education.

National High School Alliance

Institute for Educational Leadership, Washington, DC   20008
(202) 822-9405 • fax: (202) 872-4050
e-mail: hsalliance@iel.org
Web site: www.hsalliance.org

The National High School Alliance is a partnership of over fifty organizations. It includes a diverse cross section of perspectives. The goal of the alliance is to foster high academic achievement, close the achievement gap, and promote growth in high school quality. The Web site includes publications available for download and links to reports about high school reform, including charter schools.

Thomas B. Fordham Institute
1701 K Street NW, Suite 1000, Washington, DC   20006
(202) 223-5452 • fax: (202) 223-9226
e-mail: backtalk@edexcellence.neet
Web site: www.edexcellence.net

The Thomas B. Fordham Institute is a think tank associated with the Thomas B. Fordham Foundation, an Ohio foundation dedicated to ensuring that all children receive a quality education. The institute publishes a newsletter, *Education Gadfly* as well as a large number of books, pamphlets, and full-length studies. In addition, it provides links to major studies and to over fifty other organizations' Web sites in the area of charter schools.

U.S. Department of Education
400 Maryland Ave., Washington, DC   20202
(800) 872-5237 • fax: (202) 401 0689
Web site: www.ed.gov

The U.S. Department of Education is the chief federal office in charge of education in the United States. It maintain a comprehensive Web site and also sponsors the Educational Publications Center, accessible through the Web site; through e-mail at edpubs@inct.ed.gov; or by phone at (877) 433-7827. The Center publishes *Innovations in Education, ED Newsletters,* and *Helping Your Child,* among others. Full reports can be ordered free of charge.

WestEd
730 Harrison Street, San Francisco, CA   94107
(415) 565-3000 • fax: (415) 565-3012
Web site: www.wested.org

WestEd is a non-profit research, advocacy, and resource center devoted to the education of underserved children. WestEd operates an e-mail newsletter and news notification service free of charge and also provides links to articles and other publications. As a part of its mission, it is one of three sponsors of the U.S. Charter Schools Web site at www.uscharterschools.org. This is a comprehensive site for information on charter schools.

Bibliography

Books

Scott Franklin Abernathy — *No Child Left Behind and the Public Schools.* Ann Arbor: University of Michigan Press, 2007.

Scott Franklin Abernathy — *School Choice and the Future of American Democracy.* Ann Arbor: University of Michigan Press, 2006.

Jeanne Allen and David Heffernan — *Charter Schools Today: Changing the Face of American Education.* Washington, DC: Center for Education Reform, 2006.

Mark Berends — *Charter School Outcomes.* New York: Erlbaum, 2007.

Julian R. Betts and Tom Loveless — *Getting Choice Right: Ensuring Equity and Efficiency in Education Policy.* Washington, DC: Brookings Institution Press, 2005.

Gerald W. Bracey — *Setting the Record Straight: Responses to Misconceptions About Public Education in the U.S.* Portsmouth, NH: Heinemann, 2004.

Jack Buckley and Mark Schneider — *Charter Schools: Hope or Hype?* Princeton, NJ: Princeton University Press, 2007.

Katrina E. Bulkley and Priscilla Wohlstetter
Taking Account of Charter Schools: What's Happened and What's Next? New York: Teachers College Press, 2004.

Martin Carnoy, et al.
The Charter School Dust-Up. New York: Teachers College Press, 2005.

Kevin P. Chavous
Serving Our Children: Charter Schools and the Reform of American Public Education. Sterling, VA: Capital Books, 2004.

Peter W. Cookson and Kristina Berger
Expect Miracles: Charter Schools and the Politics of Hope and Despair. Boulder, CO: Westview Press, 2004.

Ronald G. Corwin and Joe Schneider
The Charter School Hoax: Fixing America's Schools. Lanham, MD: Rowman & Littlefield, 2007.

Terrence E. Deal, et al.
Adventures of Charter School Creators: Leading from the Ground Up. Lanham, MD: Scarecrow Education, 2004.

David Dunn, et al.
Charter High Schools: Closing the Achievement Gap. Washington, DC: U.S. Department of Education, 2006.

Frederick M. Hess
Urban School Reform: Lessons from San Diego. Cambridge, MA: Harvard Education Press, 2005.

Paul T. Hill
Charter Schools Against the Odds. Stanford, CA: Education Next Books, 2006.

Lance T. Izumi   *Free to Learn: Lessons from Model Charter Schools*. San Francisco: Pacific Research Institute, 2005.

Joanne Jacobs   *Our School: The Inspiring Story of Two Teachers, One Big Idea, and the School that Beat the Odds*. New York: Palgrave Macmillan, 2005.

Carol Klein   *Virtual Charter Schools and Home Schooling*. Youngstown, NY: Cambria Press, 2006.

Myron Lieberman   *The Educational Morass: Overcoming the Stalemate in American Education*. Lanhan, MD: Rowman & Littlefield Education, 2007.

Anne Turnbaugh Lockwood   *The Charter Schools Decade*. Lanham, MD: Scarecrow Education, 2004.

James William Noll   *Taking Sides: Clashing Views on Controversial Educational Issues*. Dubuque, IA: McGraw-Hill/Dushkin, 2006.

Harry Anthony Patrinos   *Mobilizing the Private Sector for Public Education: A View from the Trenches*. Washington, DC: World Bank, 2007.

Paul E. Peterson   *Choice and Competition in American Education*. Lanham, MD: Rowman & Littlefield, 2006.

Janelle T. Scott   *School Choice and Diversity: What the Evidence Says*. New York: College Teachers Press, 2005.

Doug Thomas   *"The Coolest School in America": How Small Learning Communities Are Changing Everything.* Lanham, MD: Scarecrow Education, 2005.

Lawrence D. Weinberg   *Religious Charter Schools: Legalities and Practicalities.* Charlotte, NC: Information Age, 2007.

Ron W. Zimmer and Richard J. Buddin   *Making Sense of Charter Schools: Evidence from California.* Santa Monica, CA: Rand, 2006.

Periodicals

Achiever   "What Is the Difference between Charter Schools and Other Public Schools?"October 2006.

Ulrich Boser   "Getting Down to Business," *Teacher Magazine*, March–April 2007.

Jack Buckley and Mark Schneider   "Are Charter School Students Harder to Educate? Evidence from Washington, DC," *Educational Evaluation & Policy Analysis*, Winter 2005.

Jack Buckley and Mark Schneider   "Are Charter School Parents More Satisfied with Schools? Evidence from Washington, DC," *Peabody Journal of Education*, Winter 2006..

Marcia Clemmitt   "Fixing Urban Schools: Has No Child Left Behind Helped Minority Students? The Issues," *CQ Researcher*, April 17, 2007.

Marjorie Coeyman — "Charter Schools Build on a Decade of Experimentation," *Christian Science Monitor*, January 7, 2003.

Dale DeCesare and Amy Berk Anderson — "Charter Law 'Fix': A Mistake," *Denver Post*, October 1, 2006.

Alan Dessoff — "Mixed Reviews: Educational Leaders and Politicians Debate the Effectiveness of Charter Schools," *District Administrator*, July 2006.

Naomi Dillon — "Breaking District Boundaries to Get Kids in a School," *Education Digest*, March 2007.

Josh Dunn and Martha Derthick — "Courts and Choice: Testing the Constitutionality of Charters and Vouchers," *Education Next*, Spring 2007.

Mary Bailey Estes — "Charter Schools: Do They Work for Troubled Students?" *Preventing School Failure*, Fall 2006.

Chester E. Finn Jr. — "All Aboard the Charters?" *National Review*, October 9, 2006.

Elissa Gootman — "Public vs. Charter Schools: A New Debate," *New York Times*, April 5, 2006.

Jennifer Hancock — "Why Humanist Communities Should Embrace Charter Schools," *Humanist*, September–October 2005.

R.C. Heaggans "Unpacking Charter Schools: A Knapsack Filled with Broken Promises," *Education*, Spring 2006.

Luis A. Huerta, et al. "Cyber Charter Schools," *Phi Delta Kappan*, January 2006.

Thomas Hutton "Five Big Questions (and Many Smaller Ones) Your Board Should Ask Before Authorizing a Charter School," *American School*, 2007.

Indianapolis Star "Charter Schools Draw the Most Rookie Teachers,"August 20, 2006

Marci Kanstoroom "Looking in the Wrong Place: The Flaw in the New Federal Charter School Study," *Education Next*, Fall 2005.

Katherine Kersten "Cross Country: Don't Protest, Just Shop Somewhere Else," *Wall Street Journal*, March 2, 2006.

Anne Kibbler "Plan for Virtual Charter Schools Creates Concern," *Herald-Times*, March 27, 2007.

Anne C. Lewis "Promises to Keep," *Phi Delta Kappan*, January 2007.

Dan Lips and Evan Feinberg "Charting a Course Toward Better Education," *USA Today*, March 2007.

Dan Lips and Evan Feinberg "School Choice: A Progress Report," *USA Today*, January 2007.

Vicki McClure and Mary Shanklin — "Risky Choices," *Orlando Sentinel*, March 25, 2007.

Erika Mellon — "Can HISD Copy Success of Charter Schools? Longer Day Plan Might Work, But It Would Cost the District Millions," *Houston Chronicle*, April 29, 2007.

Ronald J. Newell — "Growing Hope as a Determinant of School Effectiveness," *Phi Delta Kappan*, February 2007.

Michael Petrelli — "Identity Crisis: Can Charter Schools Survive Accountability?," *Education Next*, Summer 2005.

"Reining In Charter Schools" — *New York Times*, May 10, 2006.

Greg Richmond — "Piecing Together the Charter Puzzle," *Education Week*, April 18, 2007.

Cynthia Rigg — "Progress Report: Charter Schools," *Crain's New York Business*, March 5, 2007.

Erik W. Robelen — "Advocates Want Bigger Role for Charters Under NCLB," *Education Week*, April 18, 2007.

Andrew J. Rotherman — "Virtual Schools, Real Innovation," *New York Times*, April 7, 2006.

Karen Rutzick — "Virtual Reality Check," *Teacher Magazine*, March–April 2007.

Michael W. Simpson	"The Charter School as Factory: This Is Reform?" *Essays in Education*, Fall 2003.
Nelson Smith	"Charters as a Solution?" *Education Next*, Winter 2007.
Dirk Tillotson	"What's Next for New Orleans," *High School Journal*, December 2006.
Washington Times	"Bolster Charter Schools," August 29, 2005.
Joe Williams	"Games Charter Opponents Play: How Local School Boards—and their Allies—Block the Competition," *Education Next*, Winter 2007.
Priscilla Wohlstetter and Joanna Smith	"Improving Schools Through Partnerships: Learning from Charter Schools," *Phi Delta Kappan*, February 2006.
Caprice Young	"Empowering Teachers and Parents with Charter Schools Can Bring New Opportunities to Urban Communities," *UrbanEd*, Fall–Winter 2005.

Internet Resources

The Center for Policy Studies and Hamline University, Education Evolving	"Staying In!!! Youth Once on the Path to Quitting School Explain Why Motivation Is Central to Learning and Graduating" April 2007. www.educationevolving.org.
Charter Schools	National Education Association, 2007. www.nea.org.

Ed.gov,
U.S. Department
of Education

"Remarks of Secretary Spelling at the 2007 National Charter Schools Conference", 2007. www.ed.gov.

Guilbert C.
Hentschke, et al.

"Trends and Best Practices for Education Management Organizations," Policy Perspectives, WestEd, 2003. www.WestEd.org.

Robin J. Lake and
Paul T. Hill, eds.

Hopes, Fears, and Reality: A Balanced Look at American Charter Schools in 2006, Center on Reinventing Public Education, 2006. www.ecs.org.

Bettie
Landauer-
Menchauer

"How Segregated Are Michigan's Schools? Changes in Enrollment from 1992–93 to 2004–2005," The Education Policy Center, Michigan State University, February 2006. www.epc.msu.edu.

Gary Miron and
Brooks Applegate

"Teacher Attrition in Charter Schools," Great Lakes Center for Education Research and Practice, Education Public Interest Center, May 2007. epsl.asu.edu.

National Alliance
for Public Charter
Schools

"Creating the Schools Our Nation Needs: NCLB Reauthorization and the Promise of Charter Schools," March 2007. www.publiccharters.org.

F. Howard Nelson
and Nancy
Van Meter

"Charter School Achievement on the 2005 Assessment of Educational Progress," American Federation of Teachers, November 2005. www.aft.org.

Isaiah J. Poole   "Rain on the Charter School Parade,"
                       TomPaine.common sense, August 23,
                       2006. www.tompaine.com.

Todd Ziebarth   "Peeling the Lid Off State-Imposed
                       Charter School Caps," Issue Brief,
                       National Alliance for Public Charter
                       Schools, February 2007.
                       www.publiccharterschools.org

Index